M. I. HUMMEL.

THE GOLDEN ANNIVERSARY ALBUM

Portfolio Press / A Robert Campbell Rowe Book

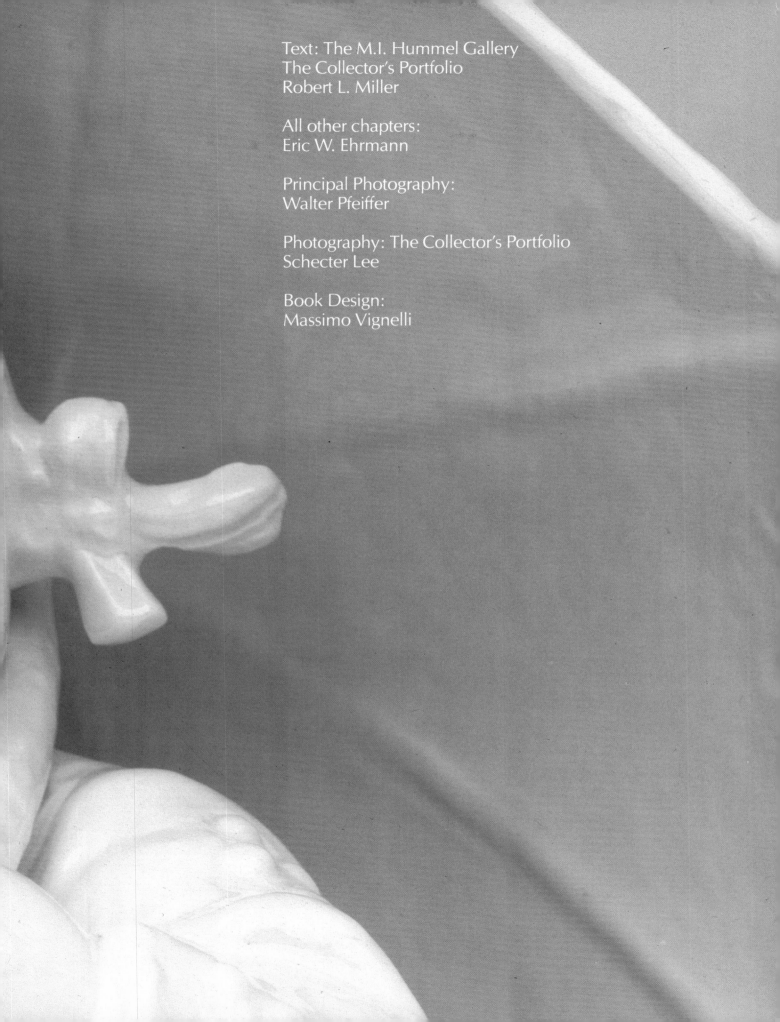

Text: The M.I. Hummel Gallery
The Collector's Portfolio
Robert L. Miller

All other chapters:
Eric W. Ehrmann

Principal Photography:
Walter Pfeiffer

Photography: The Collector's Portfolio
Schecter Lee

Book Design:
Massimo Vignelli

Library of Congress Catalog Card Number 84-61300
ISBN 0-942620-08-9

Printed and bound by Amilcare Pizzi, S.p.A., Milan, Italy

CONTENTS

M.I.Hümmel

The Golden
Anniversary
Album

Goebel

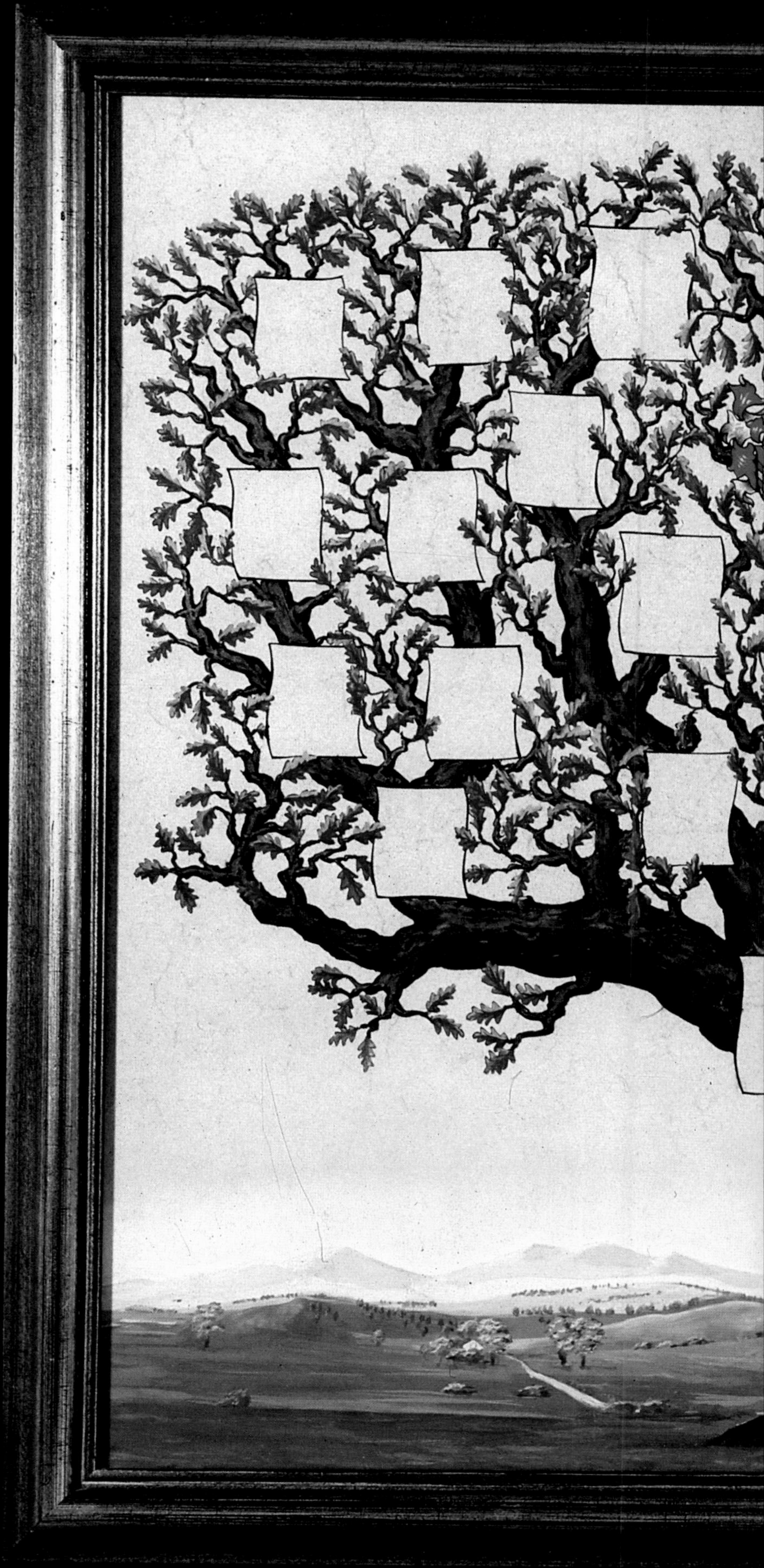

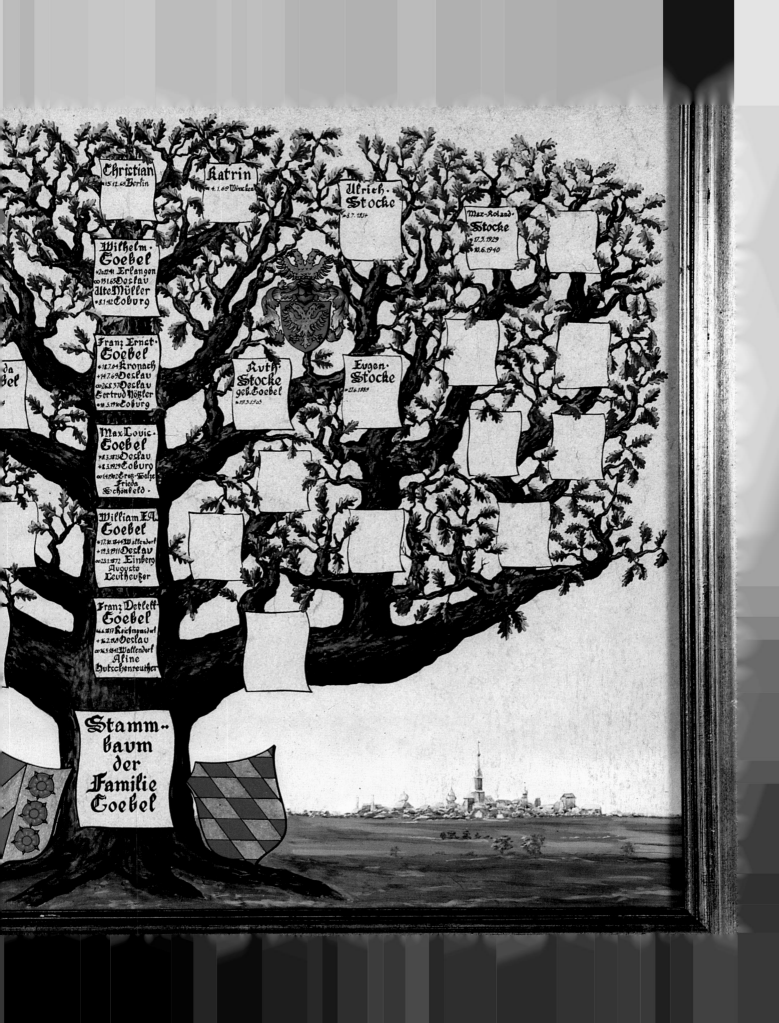

Georg Wilhelm von Göbel
Hofrath und Hofbuchdrucker
geb. 17.2.1619
zu Mannheim
gest. 1688

Johann Friedrich von Göbel
Buchdrucker zu Mannheim
geb. 11.6.1660 · gest. Ende 1695

Georg Wilhelm Göbel
Kammerpräsident zu Coburg
geb. 28.1.1696 in Mannheim
gest. 26.7.1776 in Coburg
1.Ehe, Eve Barbara Schwarz, 2.Ehe
mit Friederike, Sophie Bechmann

Schloß Wespenstein

Juliane Helene, geb. Gräf
geb. 7.2.1755 · Gräfenthal
gest. April 1834, dem Ehepaar
wurden auf Schloß Wespenstein 9 Kinder geboren.

**Amtmann und Hofrath
Johann, Gottfried, Göbel**
geb. 7.12.1744 in Hildburghausen
gest. 11.4.1817. Schloß Wespenstein

Friederike, geb. Faber
geb. 31.3.1797 zu Stelzen
gest. 11.4.1818 · Reichmannsdorf

Christian, Friedrich Göbel
Oberförster
geb. 21.4.1778 · Gräfenthal, Thür.
Schloß Wespenstein
gest. 11.4.1818 in Reichmannsdorf

Johanne, Aline geb. Hutschenreuther
geb. 20.2.1826 in Wallendorf
gest. 2.10.1907, in Oeslau

Franz Harro, Detleff Goebel
Kaufmann
geb. 6.6.1817, in Reichmannsdorf
gest. 16.2.1909 in Oeslau

Auguste, geb. Leutheuser
geb. 18.9.1846 in Oeslau
gest. 10.3.1897 in Oeslau

**Kommerzienrat
Friedrich Adolph, William Goebel**
Kaufmann
geb. 17.10.1844 in Wallendorf
gest. 19.3.1911 in Oeslau

Bertha, Frieda geb. Schönfeld
geb. 10.9.1880 in Magdeburg
gest. 17.9.1958 in Coburg

**Kommerzienrat
Max, Louis, Gustav Goebel**
geb. 8.3.1873 in Oeslau
gest. 8.3.1929 in Coburg

1985 marks the fiftieth anniversary of the introduction of the first M.I. Hummel figurines to the public. Over these past five decades, millions of people around the world have come to know and love them.

The figurines represent a golden alliance between the late artist, Sister Maria Innocentia Hummel, and *W. Goebel Porzellanfabrik* in West Germany, the translators of her two-dimensional art into the figurines that are so deeply appreciated.

The purpose of this book is to help celebrate the anniversary of this alliance. We have created it in album form so that we may share in words and pictures the history and highlights of fifty years of M.I. Hummel figurines, just as though this were a family album.

We take pride in our family spirit at Goebel. Many of our staff are continuing their families' traditions at our company. And there is very much a spirit of family surrounding the M.I. Hummel figurines. The idea for them was developed by my father, Franz, who worked directly with Sister Maria Innocentia. Today, we at Goebel carry on the tradition he began, working directly with the members of the Franciscan order, to whom Sister Maria Innocentia devoted, and assigned, the creations of her convent time. And we are confident that future generations will continue what was begun so long ago.

It is worth noting that the Goebel company was not too long past its own fiftieth anniversary when the idea for creating the M.I. Hummel figurines was developed. As you will read later in this book, those were difficult years for everyone. It was a major challenge to successfully introduce a new line of figurines in the midst of a terrible worldwide depression and, after a devastating war, to ultimately succeed in bringing them to the attention of the public.

In many ways, life is easier today than it was fifty years ago. But modern life with its urban orientation and emphasis on automation and technology creates a nostalgic longing for certain aspects of the past. There can be no doubt that one of the reasons for the immense popularity of Sister Maria Innocentia's art is her imagery of children in a more carefree time. They are children who inspire happiness, who fill us with glad feelings. And that is our ambition with this album: to bring alive the joy known to so many millions who love M.I. Hummel figurines.

I hope it will bring you much pleasure.

Wilhelm Goebel

Wilhelm Goebel
Rödental, Bavaria,
Federal Republic of Germany
June, 1984

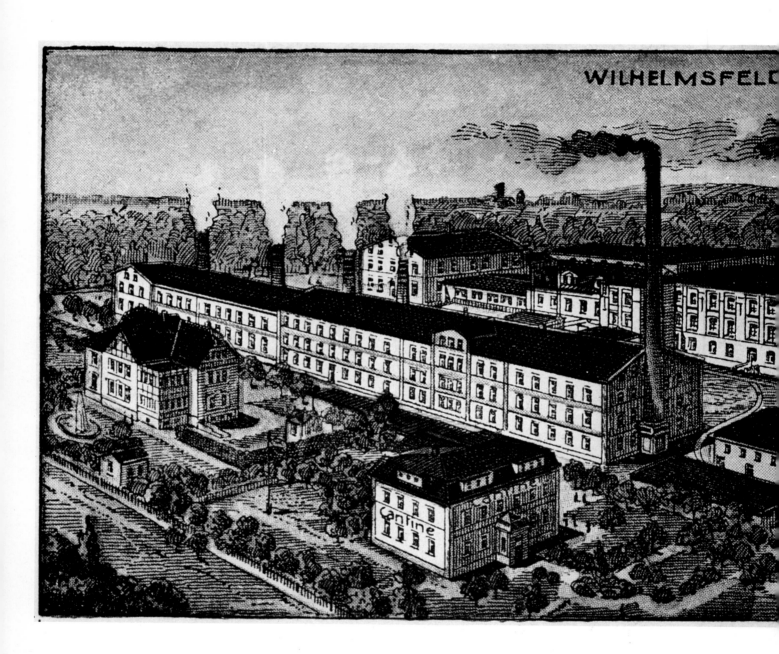

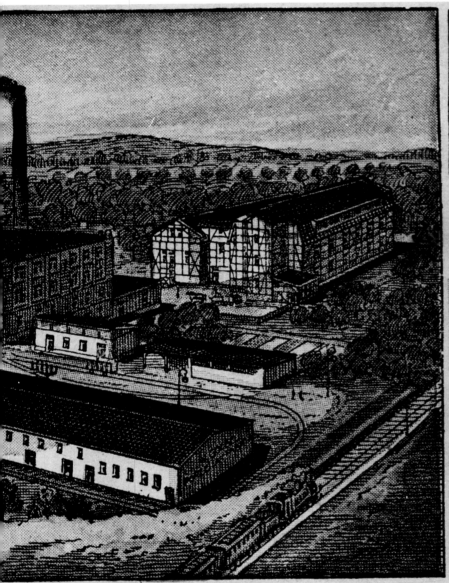

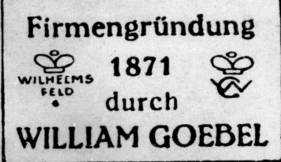

Firmengründung
WILHELMS FELD
1871
durch
WILLIAM GOEBEL

Arbeiter wohnhaus Augustenfeld.

Das alte Kontor.

Right: Franz Goebel as a young boy, around 1908.

Below: This turn-of-the-century advertisement promoted Goebel products at the Leipzig Trade Fair by using a jugendstil (art nouveau) design theme.

Overleaf: During the late-19th and early-20th centuries Goebel was a leader in the manufacturing of affordable collector pieces based on both traditional, and contemporary designs. Many of these pieces reflect the Meissen tradition and were an important part of Goebel's effort to offer high-class design at a popular price.

Franz Goebel's Challenge

America had always held a special place in the heart of Franz Goebel. As a young man in the early 1920's, he was sent to the United States by his father, Max-Louis, to learn the American porcelain and ceramic art market. It was the era of prosperity, the Jazz Age. But back in Germany it was a dismal time. There was runaway inflation, political chaos, and even Franz Goebel's hometown of Coburg, insulated from the brunt of these developments in a remote corner of northern Bavaria, was beginning to feel the pinch. Franz knew that his father would have to expand the export markets of the *W. Goebel Porzellanfabrik* considerably to avoid the economic uncertainty that was plaguing the German nation.

"Max-Louis had a motto," Trude Goebel, Franz's wife, recalls. "'The world is my market.' This motto was passed on to Franz at an early age. He traveled to the United States and Canada and returned with a head full of ideas for new products. He came home with a firm grasp of the meaning of his father's words."

By the turn of the century the name Goebel had already been well established in the United States as a manufacturer of porcelain dinnerware, dolls and decorative ceramic objects of high quality. An important part of the company's production was destined for the American market.

Max-Louis, who had taken over the business in 1914 from his father, William, was a productive, innovative man. It was Max-Louis' intention to capture a larger share of the important overseas market through the introduction of new products, and he pursued this goal so avidly that he became known by his customers as the one to watch. American buyers would always stop at the Goebel booth at the annual Leipzig Trade Fair to see what new developments Goebel had in store for them. And more often than not they would leave behind substantial orders for Goebel products.

In spite of Max-Louis' success, by the 1920's the pressure was on to expand export markets in order to bring in the badly needed hard currencies required for economic survival. The faltering *Reichsmark* was nearly worthless, and it was not unusual to pay a wheelbarrow's worth of the currency for a two-pound loaf of black bread.

In 1926, Max-Louis, along with young Franz, now back from his travels developed a line of competitively priced ceramic figurines that sold well on the international market. This modest success kept the Goebel factory humming in Oeslau, just outside Coburg. The four hundred workers of the firm were spared the tough times that had set in around the nation.

When Max-Louis Goebel died in 1929, it was up to Franz to carry on the legacy of his father, developing new products and expanding overseas markets. With his brother-in-law, Dr. Eugen Stocke, a Heidelberg-trained economist, running the financial side of the business, Franz was free to implement the ideas he had developed during his stay in North America.

"My father spent a great deal of time studying the American market," remembers Wilhelm Goebel, Franz's son and the current chairman of Goebel, who represents the fifth generation of his family. "He spent time in London and Paris as well. But he had a gut feeling about America being the greatest market in the world, and as a result of this feeling he set out to develop a series of ceramic figures that everyone could afford and enjoy."

As he looked back at the history of porcelain and figurine making, Franz Goebel came to the realization that the form of the child had yet to see its day. The image of the child in porcelain had developed, in large part, as the result of renaissance religious art and, to a lesser extent, during the baroque and rococo periods. Children took the form of angels and cherubs and little, if any, emphasis had ever been placed on the contemporary child as the subject of fine ceramic figurines. In sharp contrast, the German toy and doll industry, the world's largest, centered in Nürnberg, only sixty-five miles south of the Goebel porcelain factory, was having great success with just such motifs.

"Franz wanted to develop a series of figurines that would be more than just decorative pieces," remembers Dr. Stocke, eighty-nine years old at the time of this interview (1984). "He wanted to create something that would open people's eyes and bring out their feelings. He wanted to produce figurines that could make you smile and think back on your own childhood days. And it is no secret that for most of us, our childhood days are our most memorable times."

Children had long occupied a traditional place as subjects in German literature, as far back as the *Märchen* (folk tales) that had been passed along from generation to generation by work of mouth, and had developed into collections such as *Grimm's Fairy Tales*. These stories almost always offered a moral, a piece of folk wisdom, or a moment of reflection. They were helpful to parents bringing up children, for they offered imaginative lessons that could be applied to daily life, and when read aloud they fostered a particular family closeness; they inspired scenes of parent and child huddled around a fireplace, or of children being tucked into bed at night. The themes came from the German countryside, with the most typically prominent being *Hansel and Gretel*. They offered warmth, innocence and make-believe. By the time Franz Goebel set out to make his figurines, these tales were popular the world over.

Franz had now established his goal. In 1933, he started his search for the art and artist whose work was suitable for transformation into three-dimensional figurines.

Discovery in Munich

Munich in the early 1930's was a showplace for the decorative arts. In spite of the economic difficulties facing Germany, the department stores and specialty shops of the Bavarian capital put on a proud face, displaying fine dinnerware, figurines, and decorative pieces manufactured by the great names in German porcelain.

But Munich, the major Catholic center of southern Germany, was a focal point for religious art as well. Shops featuring Oberammergau woodcarvings, lithographed icons, and religious books and cards dotted the city, catering to the local population as well as to the tourists who wished to take home fine examples of Bavarian religious art. When Franz traveled to Munich to see how his products were doing during the Christmas season of 1933, a round of visits to these religious art shops was high on his list.

"As always, Franz was looking for ways to expand our market," Dr. Stocke recalls. "Our Munich representative recommended that he visit some of the establishments that featured religious art so that he could gain some perspective in this area. And, of course, he did."

Franz visited several religious art shops, along with his Munich sales representative, Ernst Steiner. What was discovered during one of these visits was the first milestone: the art that would one day bring joy and happiness into the hearts of millions of people. On the counter of a small religious art shop in Munich were displayed the art cards of Sister Maria Innocentia Hummel.

"Franz was an extremely emotional person, a man who acted on instinct," Dr. Stocke says. "His reaction to the art cards of Sister Maria Innocentia Hummel was one of instant enthusiasm. Here were wonderful sketches of innocent children, drawn by a Franciscan Sister. They were exactly what he was looking for to transform into figurines."

Franz returned home to Coburg for Christmas, carrying with him a few of the art cards, which were printed color reproductions based upon Sister Maria Innocentia's original paintings. In keeping with tradition at the Goebel factory, the Goebel and Stocke families honored their employees with a gala Christmas party. Goebel products had experienced a modest upturn in holiday sales, and new orders for the coming year were a true godsend. But as Franz shook the hands of his employees and wished them well for the holidays, he kept the gladdest tidings of all to himself. His mind was working on the concept of what have come to be known as the M.I. Hummel figurines.

The Technical Challenge

Franz discussed the artwork of Sister Maria Innocentia with his two top modelers, Arthur Möller and Reinhold Unger. These men, master sculptors, studied Sister Maria Innocentia's cards and considered the ways in which the two-dimensional artwork could be transformed into three-dimensional figurines. When Franz received their report he was not surprised. It would be the most challenging project ever undertaken by the Goebel factory.

"Not only would the project be technically challenging, it would be challenging from the financial side as well," Dr. Stocke says. "The cost of starting up production would be staggering. But Franz was so confident of his idea that he said we should do 'whatever it takes.' He went ahead and wrote to Sister Maria Innocentia at the Siessen Convent asking for permission to use her art."

The strength of his feelings and of his personal commitment to creating three-dimensional figurines from the artwork of Sister Maria Innocentia is made obvious through a letter to her dated December 19, 1934.

> *Dear Sister Hummel,*
> *I was pleased to hear that you have assured me the permission to interpret your artwork in porcelain, ceramic and other three-dimensional mediums. I am very enthusiastic about your artwork, and I see many advantages if your artwork/drawings could be rendered in three-dimensional form. In any case, the three-dimensional renderings must be of the highest quality, in order to bring the nuances of your wonderful characterizations to figurine form.*
>
> *I give you the utmost assurance that those of your works which I am given permission to manufacture into figurines will receive my best attention and the knowledge of all my years in the porcelain business. I will employ the best production techniques my factory can offer in order to bring a truly beautiful product onto the market, a product that will always be an honor to its artist and designer.*
>
> *My figurines, like your drawings, will appear with your signature.*

During 1935 Franz Goebel worked closely with his two master sculptors, Arthur Möller (top) and Reinhold Unger (above), to develop the first Goebel figurines based on Sister Maria Innocentia Hummel's art.

I, personally, will always be watching over the quality control to ensure that only the best pieces will be brought into commerce.
I would be pleased to send you samples in white of figurines based on your artwork so that you could advise me on their decoration. In this way, the figurines would best reflect your wishes and spirit.
Sincerely,
Franz Goebel

(Excerpted and paraphrased translation)

On January 7th, 1935 Franz Goebel received the following reply:

Dear Mr. Goebel,
I agree to allow your firm the right to create three-dimensional figures based on my drawings, but only if I may see these works appear under my name, and can control the quality of the manufacture.
Sincerely,
M.I. Hummel

(Excerpted and paraphrased translation)

Franz Goebel responded to the letter of Sister Maria Innocentia on January 9, 1935.

Dear Sister Hummel,
Of course, I am ready and eager to allow you to inspect the quality of each and every piece created from your artwork before I place it on sale.
Franz Goebel

(Excerpted and paraphrased translation)

Franz was ecstatic, and eager to meet the technical challenges of the new project. He assembled an expert team of craftsmen whose time and efforts were consecrated to the pioneering of the M.I. Hummel figurines. Special paints had to be prepared, and endless hours were spent experimenting with a variety of porcelain and ceramic bodies and glazes, in order to find those that would best lend themselves to the nuances of Sister Maria Innocentia's art.

The training Franz had received at the State School for Porcelain and Ceramics at Bunzlau was a demanding curriculum that covered all aspects of manufacturing, from the chemistry of the various porcelain and ceramic bodies to modeling, moldmaking, painting and glazing. Now, Franz put that training into action, as he supervised every step of the process that led to the first sample models of the M.I. Hummel figurines. He had one goal in mind: to create figurines of the highest quality that would meet with the approval of Sister Maria Innocentia and the Siessen Convent so that he could display them at the Leipzig Trade Fair in March, 1935.

"Most of our customers knew Franz as a promoter," Dr. Stocke recalls, "but in his heart, Franz Goebel was very much a *porzelliner* in the Bavarian-Thuringian tradition. He wasn't afraid to roll up his sleeves and get involved in the actual figurine-making process because he was a

FORMEREI

Early production was often a painstaking trial-and-error experience. Among the pieces from this early production are many with variations. The process included (clockwise from top left): Filling the old round charcoal heated kiln, 1937; Enamel firing, 1937; Glazing by hand, 1936; Mold making, 1935; Master painter Louis Knauer at work, 1936; Assembling a figurine, 1937.

The ever-popular Merry Wanderer was one of the first M.I. Hummel figurines manufactured by Goebel. It has come to symbolize the universal appeal of the figurines, and the artwork of Sister Maria Innocentia, from which they are developed.

team player. And if there was ever a time for teamwork, it was then."

The development of the first models of the M.I. Hummel figurines was a virtual race against time. Modelers Möller and Unger, entrusted with the responsibility of sculpting the figurines to the likeness of Sister Maria Innocentia's drawings, worked long into the nights. More often than not, Franz was at their sides, making helpful suggestions and offering that pair of eyes so often vital to the creative process.

The painters painstakingly applied the specially mixed colors to the first models. A few pieces were cast in porcelain, but both the Goebel and Stocke families, along with modelers Möller and Unger, decided that an earthenware body was the best medium for the three-dimensional renditions of Sister Maria Innocentia's art.

"When we finished a group of sample production pieces we would put them on a table and Franz Goebel, his mother, Frieda, Dr. Stocke, and his wife, Rut, (Franz Goebel's sister), would inspect each piece," recalls Fritz Hellmond, a retired painter who was active at that time. "They would compare each figurine with examples of Sister Maria Innocentia's artwork. Only those figurines that conformed best to her original sketches would be chosen to go to the Siessen Convent for final approval."

Soon, individual models of figurines — which came to be known as *Puppy Love, Little Fiddler, Book Worm, Strolling Along, Sensitive Hunter, Merry Wanderer, Begging His Share,* and *Flower Madonna* — were ready to be presented to the Siessen Convent for approval. All of the Goebel craftsmen involved in the project had responded to the challenge by achieving a new level of technical competence that helped raise the standard for everyone at the factory.

"From the beginning the figurines were something special to all of us," recalls Erich Popp, a retired supervisor in the casting department who was active in the early development of the M.I. Hummel figurines. "We all had to learn new techniques very quickly. And in order to do this we developed a true spirit of teamwork, a spirit that has been passed from one generation of Goebel craftsmen to another and is very much alive today."

Leipzig, March, 1935

The seasonally-held Leipzig Trade Fair was the focal point for European and American retail and distribution firms seeking contact with German manufacturers. These fairs were the most important sales events of the year for most German manufacturers because they gave them a clear indication of what their export business was going to be. And in an export-oriented economy such as Germany's, a successful week at Leipzig was, for many companies, often the difference between profit and loss, between keeping workers on the payroll and laying them off. A successful fair meant being able to develop a new product and launch it on the international marketplace. With the enormous risk the company had taken in the development and first production of the M.I. Hummel figurines, success at Leipzig was imperative for Goebel.

This was the era of "steamship commerce." American businessman en route to Leipzig would spend six or seven days on the grand liners — plenty of time to fraternize with colleagues from around the country about trends, prices, and what they had on their shopping lists. Thanks to the tradition of manufacturing new and novel products established by Max-Louis Goebel, many of the important American businessman were always eager to visit the Goebel display at the Leipzig Trade

Fair. They could always count on finding new and exciting gift and tableware products. Now Franz was following in his father's tradition of innovation and what he had in store for visitors to the Leipzig Trade Fair would be quite a surprise indeed.

Coburg was a favorite stopping-off place for American businessmen on their way to Europe's largest trade fair. Often they were invited to stop by the Goebel factory for a "sneak preview" of the year's new products and to spend time with Franz and Dr. Stocke, talking business and enjoying the fine food and wine of the region. So, by the time of the March, 1935 fair, there were already rumblings in Leipzig that an important new Goebel product would be making its debut.

"We had a good number of orders for our first M.I. Hummel figurines displayed at Leipzig in March of 1935. They could be given as gifts, or as collector items," Dr. Stocke remembers. "The Americans liked them because Sister Maria Innocentia's themes offered a refreshing departure from almost everything on the U.S. market at that time. The figurines were a genuinely new product. But while we had gained some acceptance for the line, it was clear to both Franz and me that the market would not develop overnight." Still, business was good enough to warrant Franz Goebel's asking Sister Maria Innocentia for the right to produce additional figurines based on her artwork. And in August, 1935, Franz made his first visit to the Siessen Convent.

By the end of 1935, Goebel had released several more figurines, expanding the collection through HUM 46. (The HUM number refers to the listing of each design in the Goebel production journal; the same number can also be found incised on the bottom of each figurine base for easy identification.) These original models include some of the most sought-after figurines among collectors today.

Quality is Rewarded

The modest success of the first M.I. Hummel figurines gave Goebel some financial breathing room at a time when many porcelain manufacturers were experiencing severe financial hardship, or even having to dissolve. Then, too, the standard of production achieved through the manufacture of the M.I. Hummel figurines created a new goal of excellence to strive for at Goebel.

"The key to the whole operation was and continues to be the quality control," says retired porcelain painter Fritz Hellmond. "I remember when Franz Goebel's mother, Frieda, would personally examine each piece before it was sent to the packing department to make sure that it was suitable for sale. Examples like hers encouraged all of us to develop a 'sixth sense' for quality so that the production of the M.I. Hummel figurines became a family affair."

Sales of M.I. Hummel figurines on the international market during the 1935 Christmas season were brisk. Marshall Field & Co., the famous Chicago department store, which had placed an important order in March, reported an enthusiastic response to the new Goebel product. Responding to the upbeat projections of Marshall Field and other retailers, Franz Goebel asked for, and received, permission to launch fifteen new M.I. Hummel figurines on the market for the 1936 Christmas season, HUM 47 through 62.

Sister Maria Innocentia and her assistant Sister Laura journeyed to the Goebel factory in August, 1936, to meet with Franz Goebel and master sculptors Möller and Unger. "News of Sister Maria Innocentia's forthcoming visit spread rapidly through the factory," remembers Emmy

Little Fiddler was another of the early pieces put into production by Franz Goebel. The Goebel family worked hand in hand with their craftsmen to help make Franz's idea a success.

Faber, a retired bookkeeper who worked closely with Franz and Dr. Stocke. "We were all deeply honored and we wanted everything to look just right. The factory and the administrative offices were always kept spotless, but in honor of her visit we all pitched in with a little extra effort. I remember helping Frau Goebel wash and starch her dining room curtains so that they would look perfect for the visit."

Dr. Stocke remembers the day particularly well. "Sister Maria Innocentia was accompanied by Sister Laura, who was also an artist. We did not plan any special welcoming celebration out of respect for the regulations of the Franciscan Order. But we knew that the visiting sisters placed special value on observing the factory, our craftsmen and their technical expertise. In particular, the sisters wanted to learn as much as possible about how figurines were made. After touring the factory, Sister Maria Innocentia and Sister Laura were introduced to my wife Rut and we invited them into our home for lunch. At this first meeting both my wife and I felt the deep sincerity and strong religious feeling radiated by Sister Maria Innocentia and her colleague. These feelings continued over the years, and were strengthened with each visit we made to the convent."

The visit of Sister Maria Innocentia to the Goebel factory made a lasting impression on the craftsmen as well. There was great concern among them that their work would not meet the stringent specifications outlined by the artist in her correspondence with Franz Goebel. They were sailing in uncharted waters, guided only by examples of Sister Maria Innocentia's art and Franz's encouragement and unswerving faith. As *porzelliners* in the true Bavarian-Thuringian tradition, they responded to the technical challenge, hoping their work would receive approval from Sister Maria Innocentia.

"It was amazing how much confidence we all gained during her visit," Otto Schindhelm, a painter's helper at the time, recalls. "Sister Maria Innocentia took the time to stop and examine each painter's work, offering a few words of quiet advice: brighten a color here, darken one there. It was a great feeling to see the figurines come to life, and an even greater one to know that our work met with her wishes."

This visit, the only one Sister Maria Innocentia is known to have made to the Goebel factory, resulted in many helpful improvements in the design of the figurines. Reports of breakage in shipping were studied during this visit and resulted in the strengthening of the designs of the figurines in question. The tradition of cooperation that grew out of this visit set the precedent for the design review process that continues between Goebel and the Siessen Convent today. Over the years, customer feedback through retailers has occasionally come up in the design reviews and has resulted in the use of brighter colors. (These refinements are the basis for many of the so-called "variations" sought by a number of today's collectors.) Always, the end goal of these design review meetings between Goebel and the Siessen Convent has been to improve the quality of the figurines that bear Sister Maria Innocentia's name.

Winds of War

Though the artwork of Sister Maria Innocentia Hummel portrayed a Germany of naive, pastoral innocence that drew its roots from the placid farmland of Lower Bavaria, the German nation under Hitler was presenting a much different image.

The Siessen Convent was facing severe hardship as the result of

Sister Maria Innocentia's love for children is quite evident in this drawing of Ulrich Stocke as a baby. The artist drew the young child for Dr. Eugen and Rut Stocke on her only visit to the Goebel factory, in August of 1936.

Sister Maria Innocentia (right) with Franz Goebel during her only visit to the Goebel factory, in the summer of 1936. Sister Laura is at the left.

policies imposed by the Nazi regime. In February, 1937, the Hitler government issued a decree that all Catholic-administered schools, as well as other private schools, would be systematically closed. This decree came as an exceptionally hard blow to Siessen, where the training of teachers was an important part of the work. Taxes to be paid by convents and religious orders were raised to exorbitant levels, with the intent of causing these institutions to suffer economic collapse. Still, in spite of the difficulties, the Siessen Convent remained open.

A first major step taken voluntarily by many Americans opposed to the policies of Nazi Germany was the economic embargo started in 1939. It effectively curtailed shipments of German products into the United States. As a result, the flow of M.I. Hummel figurines into the United States trickled to a halt.

Germany invaded Poland in 1939 and the inevitable war began. Responding to the directives of wartime industrial policy, the Goebel factory manufactured a variety of products, including insulators for communications lines, mess hall dinnerware and dinnerware for the domestic market. A small number of M.I. Hummel figurines was made during the war years, including samples of what are now known as the international M.I. Hummel figurines. These, developed from sketches by Sister Maria Innocentia of children around the world in their native dress, are the only M.I. Hummel figurines that are not typically German in their costumes. Since they were never put into full production, and only a few samples were made, they are extremely rare.

The Line Is Drawn
By the end of the war, American troops had swept across Germany, halting their advance at the Elbe River. Coburg and the Goebel factory, lying well west of the Elbe, were in the American zone of occupation. At the same time, the Soviet army had marched into Berlin, laying claim to the whole of the German capital. The United States and its allies did not want Berlin to become a Soviet-dominated city, but the Soviets wanted to use Berlin as a symbol of their victory. Negotiations at Yalta saw the American troops pull back from the Elbe, virtually handing over most of the province of Thuringia to the Soviets. In return, the Allies received control of half of Berlin, which remained surrounded by Soviet-occupied territory. Soviet armor and infantry units pulled into the town of Sonneberg, eight miles from Coburg and sat tight, waiting to see where the line would be drawn. The Goebel factory and all the people of Coburg waited, too.

"The townspeople didn't know what was going to happen to Coburg," recalls Emmy Faber. "There was the curfew, of course, and we had to be indoors by 5 o'clock in the afternoon. But we didn't really know if we were going to be on the American side of the line or the Russian side. You can't imagine what it was like those few weeks in 1945 when we were teetering on the brink of losing everything."

Finally, word came down from the American zone of occupation; the border of the Soviet zone would fall some six miles to the east outside the town of Neustadt. But Coburg was left in a pocket, cut off from its traditional lines of commercial influence, surrounded on three sides by the Soviet zone.

Healing the Wounds
With their backs up against the Iron Curtain, Franz Goebel and Dr. Eugen Stocke sought to pump some life into the economy of their badly

depressed region. The armistice in April, 1945, caused production to grind to a halt, and the Goebel factory was sitting idle. If it could not start up business soon, the factory would fall into disrepair. Gradually, the workers who had left for the war trickled back from internment camps, or from units that had lain down their arms at the front. "They were tired, depressed and hungry," Dr. Stocke remembers. "We did our best to feed them, and promised all the workers their jobs back if and when we started up production."

Fortunately for Goebel, the U.S. military government had a strong interest in developing those regions close to the border of Soviet-occupied East Germany. It was important to U.S. policy that they become economically healthy so that they could be models of capitalism's success in the dismal face of communism only a few miles away. As a result, U.S. authorities gave Goebel permission to manufacture and export M.I. Hummel figurines and other collector's items less than a year after the war's end.

Production started up slowly. Many of the master molds and models had been lost or broken during the war years, and master sculptors Möller and Unger had to remodel many of Sister Maria Innocentia's designs. They were also responsible for sculpting and modeling designs for the other Goebel figurines, giftware and dinnerware lines.

During this modeling process modifications were sometimes made that resulted in slight changes in figurine design. Many of these modifications were approved by Sister Maria Innocentia at Siessen as Goebel started up production again. As a result, collectors can find some interesting model variations among the pieces manufactured during this era. Known as "U.S. Zone" pieces, they can best be identified by the "made in U.S. Zone" mark, or a variation of it, stamped on the bottom of each figurine base.

Still, even though the wheels were turning again at Goebel, there were shortages of most of the raw materials required for production. Food was also scarce, and clothing was very hard to find. The winter of 1945-46 saw many homes without heat save for a few scraps of wood due to a lack of coal and oil.

"We had to go out into the forest and scavenge wood for heating that winter," remembers Emmy Faber. "And we needed ration cards to obtain basic groceries. There wasn't much, but everybody at the factory pulled together and helped one another."

Wood to fire the Goebel kilns was equally hard to find. Goebel employees would often venture into the countryside to search for fallen trees, cutting them up and bringing the wood back to the factory on horse-drawn wagons. During the winter the men would bring the wood back on horse-drawn sleds.

"The forest to the east of the factory is quite expansive and back in those days our men would go out on little expeditions hunting for wood for the kilns," Dr. Stocke remembers. "At the time there was an open border between East and West Germany and people could more or less cross where and when they pleased. So it was possible that some of the wood our men were bringing back came from the East. During the winter my wife and I would drive out into the forest on our sleigh and bring the men hot meals at noontime. They worked very hard, which helped get us going during a tough time."

When old customers of Franz Goebel in the United States heard that the factory had started up production they arranged for packages of basic foodstuffs to be shipped to the Coburg area for distribution to the

Like many German products manufactured after World War II, M.I. Hummel figurines were stamped with a "U.S. Zone" mark to note their orgin for export purposes.

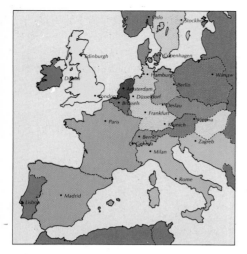

- Austria
- Belgium
- Czechoslovakia
- Denmark
- Federal Republic of Germany
- France
- German Democratic Republic
- Hungary
- Ireland
- Italy
- Netherlands
- Norway
- Poland
- Portugal
- Spain
- Sweden
- Switzerland
- United Kingdom
- Yugoslavia

townspeople. And with the lifting of the non-fraternization policy in 1946 by the United States military goverment, occupation troops could strike up friendships with German people in the towns where they were stationed. The GI's had a great deal of compassion for the people of war-torn Germany, and they helped out wherever and whenever they could.

"The American occupation troops became our greatest friends," Emmy Faber remembers. "They would give us canned meat and powdered milk. Sometimes they would bring a big truck to the Coburg town center and distribute cases of food to the population, telling us that there had been a 'truck accident.' They would say, 'we can't use it now, but you surely can.' At Goebel we had a cooperative garden and once we got things growing we started to trade fresh fruit, vegetables and eggs to the GI's for canned foodstuffs."

As relations started to normalize, the fraternization between the townspeople of Coburg and American soldiers increased. And, of course, the GI's began to see some of the early post-war M.I. Hummel figurines appear in the shops in Coburg, and throughout the U.S. occupation zone. Soon the GI's were buying the figurines of the gentle-faced children, sometimes with U.S. dollars or, occasionally, with the old inflated *Reichsmark* notes that were still being used after the war. Then, too, the soldiers found they could save their money by trading cigarettes, chocolate, nylons, chewing gum or any of the other hard-to-get items for figurines.

"The figurines really promoted goodwill between us and the Americans," remembers Gerhard Skrobek, now master sculptor for all M.I. Hummel figurines. "Franz Goebel had learned, from his travels prior to the war, that Americans love children. And now, the innocent childhood themes of Sister Maria Innocentia's designs appealed very much to the GI's, for children and dreams of the future go hand in hand."

Surely, the dreams of the future would come true; there would be a new society with a constitution modeled after that of the United States, a nation that would live in peace and prosperity, and maintain a democratic form of government. But Sister Maria Innocentia Hummel would not live to see that day, for she died in November, 1946, after a long illness. Her spirit, embodied in her art and in the M.I. Hummel figurines, would live on. (A detailed account of Sister Maria Innocentia's life appears in Chapter Five.)

In 1948 the German Federal Republic was born, and Konrad Adenauer was elected Chancellor. A new national currency was put into circulation—the *Deutsche mark*. It was as if everyone in West Germany was starting off at square one—each citizen received twenty of these new marks.

"Back then the average price of an M.I. Hummel figurine in Germany was DM 4.25—around sixty-five cents (the rate in 1948 being roughly 6 DM = $1 U.S.)," remembers Gerhard Skrobek. "That is really quite amazing. But a lot of the GI's still preferred to barter with the shopkeepers for the figurines. It was more fun for them, and it was a good way to make friends, too."

The special popularity of the M.I. Hummel figurines spread through the chain of command among the United States armed forces stationed in West Germany. Collecting the figurines provided a pastime for off-duty GI's, for officers and their wives, and for U.S. civilians as well. Recognizing this goodwill value, the American government suggested that collecting M.I. Hummel figurines was an ideal pursuit for those stationed in West Germany and went so far as to mention it in the U.S. Army's "What To Do in Germany" guide book.

As soldiers would rotate back to the United States after completing their tours of duty in Germany, their M.I. Hummel figurines would go with them, and soon the small collections begun by GI's, or by those to whom they had given the figurines, started to grow. Demand on the export market increased during the early post-war years, with the United States leading the way. Major American retailers forced to abandon sales of the M.I. Hummel figurines during the wartime embargo a decade earlier were now selling them extremely well. The great export success Franz Goebel had dreamed of when he first developed the product line began to take shape. By 1950 the Goebel factory had eight hundred employees and was humming as never before.

"Many American soldiers came to our factory," remembers Dr. Stocke. "We would allow them to tour the factory and see how the figurines were made, and at the end of the tour they were given the opportunity to buy pieces. Some soldiers would buy for themselves, others would send figurines back home to their parents or friends. Occasionally we would receive visits from high-ranking officers of the American army who were curious to find out more about our factory and the M.I. Hummel figurines."

As the first wave of American tourists came to Germany in the early 1950's there were visible signs that the quality of life was improving. Living conditions had improved markedly, and there was enough of the basic foodstuffs to go around for everybody. Coal and fuel oil were readily available, though not in large quantities, and for those who owned automobiles, there was gasoline. At Goebel, free transportation to and from work was provided by company-owned buses, and consumer products that were otherwise scarce were available to employees at reduced prices through a company-owned store. A day-care center for children was added as well as a swimming pool, sauna, and multi-purpose sports field.

"It has always been important for us to live and work as one big family," Wilhelm Goebel says. "During the first years after the war Goebel was faced with a very stiff production challenge. We always met our goals because of the harmonious relationship we maintained with our employees. The social programs are the basis for that harmony. People came from far and wide seeking employment with us, many of them coming across the border from the communist side."

Franz Goebel was not taking for granted the success of the M.I. Hummel figurines. He traveled frequently to the United States promoting the M.I. Hummel line and seeking ideas for new products. One of the things that fascinated him was the amazing success of the Walt Disney cartoon characters.

"In 1952 my father traveled to Hollywood to meet with Walt Disney," Wilhelm Goebel remembers. "It was a big occasion for him because Disney was world-famous. He returned quite pleased. Disney admired his success with the M.I. Hummel figurines, and on the strength of that success, gave Goebel the right to manufacture figurines based on some of his designs."

Goebel began manufacturing a collection of Walt Disney figurines in 1952 for distribution in the United States and other major markets. Throughout the years, production of these pieces has been limited. Today, the Goebel-Disney figurine series is the focus of a new area of

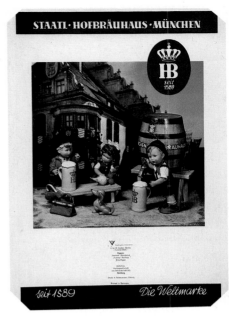

During the late 1960's American tourists were flocking to Germany. What could have been a better combination than Hofbrau and M.I. Hummel, as featured on this calendar?

Right: Franz Goebel saw great potential for the Disney images as figurines. He discussed the development of several of his new products during a 1952 visit with Walt Disney in Hollywood.

Below: The Three Little Pigs *are examples of Goebel's production of figurines based on the designs of Walt Disney characters. These and other Disney figurines had modest success during the 1950's, and are now the subject of renewed collector interest.*

collector interest because of the pieces' strong likeness to the original Walt Disney characters, as well as their relative scarcity.

The year 1952 was a very special one for Goebel in other ways. John J. McCloy, U.S. High Commissioner for Germany, visited the Goebel factory. Like many American military officers and civilian officials, McCloy was interested in seeing the textbook example of postwar reconstruction that Goebel exemplified. McCloy's goodwill visit to the factory served to underline the idea that M.I. Hummel figurine collecting was helping to promote improved German-American relations, not only with GI's stationed in West Germany but with Americans in the United States as well.

For years, Goebel, like others in the porcelain and ceramics industry, had been making figurine molds from plaster-of-paris working models. The method was fine for firms that produced many different lines of figurines in moderate numbers. But it now posed a challenge to Goebel, where demand for M.I. Hummel figurines was on the rise.

At Goebel, use of the plaster-of-paris working models was causing a slight expansion of the figurines—ten to fifteen percent beyond their designated size. In addition, some of the features, though still sharp, were losing a few of the nuances that collectors loved so much. With the demand growing across the United States as well as throughout Europe, Franz Goebel wanted to continue to stand true to his promise to Sister Maria Innocentia and the Siessen Convent to allow only figurines of the highest quality to reach the marketplace. In order to keep production level with the growing demand, Goebel had to find a way to modernize the moldmaking process.

In 1954, Gerhard Skrobek, then a young sculptor who had worked under master sculptors Unger and Möller, assumed primary responsibility for sculpting M.I. Hummel models. Skrobek had studied art at the prestigious *Reimannschule* in Berlin and, like many talented craftsmen, he was drawn to Goebel because of the excellent employment prospects during the late 1940's. Skrobek, as a sculptor, was particularly interested in the problem of mold growth.

"I set up a little lab in my kitchen and started experimenting with various materials in my spare time so that I might solve this problem of mold growth," Skrobek remembers. "In my workshop I was busy with several new figurines that had been approved for production by the Siessen Convent, and I didn't want to continue to run into the problem of having the molds expand."

Skrobek developed an acrylic resin compound that was soft and pliable like clay, but hardened to make forms that would not expand after taking several pourings of plaster of paris. This development helped revolutionize the porcelain and ceramics industry. Today, following Goebel's lead, most porcelain companies use similar resins to make their working models. Between 1954 and 1960 Goebel released many new figurines, most of them modeled by Gerhard Skrobek. With Franz Goebel's emphasis on exports and his desire to offer new M.I. Hummel figurines to a growing collector market, the acrylic resin was a timely development.

The year 1954 also marked the establishment of a "hard" border between East and West Germany. Alarmed by the mass defection of its citizens to the democratic, consumer-oriented system developing in the west, the East German government closed off its borders with West Germany. In Berlin, where it had been normal to move freely from one zone to another, the Soviets abruptly shut off their zone (comprising

The success of Goebel products helped contribute to Germany's economic miracle of the 1950's and 1960's.
Top: Franz Goebel showing his most recent products to Bavarian Minister of Economics Schedel at the 1960 Nürnberg Fair.
Middle: Federal Chancellor Ludwig Erhard examines a Goebel doll at the Nürnberg Fair.
Bottom: Franz and Wilhelm Goebel in 1968.

all of East Berlin). East German citizens and others residing in the zone were no longer permitted to enter West Berlin without special permission. The rioting that took place in East Berlin in protest of this development was put down harshly. It was a signal to the world of the Iron Curtain that had been hung across Europe. Goebel, with its factory only five miles inside the border, found itself backed up against this grim shadow of an oppressive communist system.

"Many of us lost contact overnight with friends and relatives living in the east," remembers retired painter Fritz Hellmond. "It gave us the feeling that we were cut off from our traditional region. There was nothing anyone could do in response but work harder and set an example for a new generation."

A hardened border did not slow progress at Goebel. In 1957 the U.S. Treasury designated M.I. Hummel figurines as works of art, qualifying them for reduced tariff status. By the early 1960's the company was one of the shining lights of the German economic miracle. The tall chimney of the Goebel factory could be seen miles away by East German border guards signifying that, indeed, there was another economic system on the other side of the Iron Curtain. Like the Volkswagen, M.I. Hummel figurines were more than products made in Germany. For millions, they represented friendship and goodwill between the German and American people.

Always enterprising, Franz Goebel wanted very much to expand this positive feeling in the United States toward the German people by promoting new M.I. Hummel figurines. His vehicle for doing this was a booth in the German Pavilion at the 1964 New York World's Fair, which he visited while it was being constructed. Six figurines were unveiled at the World's Fair in honor of the occasion.

"My father was amazed when he heard of the millions of people from around the world who were drawn to New York," Wilhelm Goebel remembers. "Thousands of collectors visited our exhibit and expressed an interest in the M.I. Hummel figurines. This was a factor in his decision to open his own company in the United States."

In 1969, Franz Goebel launched Hummelwerk, a distribution company in the United States, which grew out of the company Crestwick-Hummelwerk, acquired in 1959 by Goebel. Hummelwerk featured not only Goebel products, but complete lines of gift and tableware as well. The company, like its founder, earned a reputation for being promotion-minded and eager to develop new products. New collections, including Charlot Byj's *Redhead* figurines and the *Blumenkinder* by Lore, offered refreshing studies of modern children. And the gnome-like *Co-boy* series reportedly brought luck and laughter into the homes of many avid collectors. In addition, Hummelwerk helped Goebel promote a "look-alike" contest, in which parents dressed their children to resemble their favorite M.I. Hummel figurines.

Back in Germany, the Goebel factory was busy meeting the worldwide demand for its products. By 1969, the factory had a workforce of fifteen hundred and other potential employees were in training at the Bavarian State School for Ceramics at Selb. Franz Goebel's plans to develop the company into a diversified international manufacturer of dinnerware and ceramic art objects were moving along extremely well. But these plans would have to be carried on without him. Shortly before his sixty-fifth birthday in 1969, Franz Goebel died.

"We were all shocked and saddened," recalls Erich Popp, a now-retired department supervisor. "The entire factory was planning a gala celebration for him, and then suddenly he was gone. It was like a family losing its father."

It was a time for a new generation to carry on. Wilhelm Goebel and Ulrich Stocke, the son of Eugen and Rut Stocke, assumed leadership of the firm. They brought fresh blood and new ideas, and quickly made progress their number one priority. Both young men traveled frequently to the United States, spending as much as six months at a time journeying around the country to acquaint themselves with their most important market. In addition, Wilhelm had spent part of his training years at Hutschenreuther, one of Germany's largest porcelain manufacturers, where he learned the technical aspects of the porcelain and ceramics industry.

The new leadership developed new products and innovative promotional techniques that quickly gained the respect of the porcelain and giftware industry. In 1971, to mark the one hundredth anniversary of the company, Goebel entered the collector plate market with the introduction of the M.I. Hummel annual plate. The plate market was burgeoning and full of new entries, but the first M.I. Hummel plate sold out quickly, bringing the line an instant following among collectors. This series continues to be extremely popular in the United States and Canada as well as in other major markets. A further indication of its success rests with the first edition of 1971, which many dealers and collectors believe to be one of the most sought-after in plate-collecting history. Its secondary-market value has increased markedly since its year of production.

"We proved our instincts right by getting into the plate market then," says Ulrich Stocke. "Wilhelm and I were pleased that collectors were eager to acquire another form of M.I. Hummel art, but we were really quite surprised by the success of the 1971 plate."

Goebel followed up the successful launching of the annual plates with the release of new M.I. Hummel figurines. One of them, HUM 396, *Ride Into Christmas*, had become a particular favorite with collectors around holiday time, and was the design used on the 1975 annual plate.

"The popularity of *Ride Into Christmas* as both an annual plate and a figurine showed us how much collectors are interested in theme collecting," says Wilhelm Goebel. "We found that large numbers of collectors enjoyed matching the figurine to the plate. Many others collect figurines with various themes, music being one in particular. How they collect is very much an indication of their own individual feelings, their own personal expressions of how they enjoy Sister Maria Innocentia's art. All this gave us an awareness of the depths of collecting, and suggested to us that it would be a good idea to start a club for collectors, and develop their interests even further."

The Goebel Collectors' Club was established in 1977, with the purpose of providing collectors with a forum to discuss all aspects of Goebel collectibles. The first organization of its kind, the Club has been a pioneer in educating collectors about the figurine-making process, largely through information contained in its quarterly newsletter. Because of knowledge gained by Goebel through the Club, the company now sponsors tours of Goebel craftsmen around the United States, produces films and publishes a great deal of information about M.I. Hummel figurines and other collectibles. Located in a stately old mansion in historic Tarrytown, New York, the Goebel Collectors' Club has a current membership of nearly two hundred thousand.

"We've developed a wide range of programs that reach out to

Overleaf: Over the years Goebel's M.I. Hummel figurines and wildlife sculptures have become symbols of goodwill as well as valued collector items for international political leaders and a broad scope of prominent individuals.

Below: Franz Goebel always wanted to be in tune with the times. He developed a series of Beatle figurines during the 1960's at the height of the "Fab Four's" success. Pictured is John Lennon.

Dr. Eugen Stocke greets King Karl Gustaf and Queen Sylvia of Sweden on their 1983 visit to Coburg.

Former President Ford accepts a Goebel eagle at a 1977 ceremony. U.S. Ambassador Burns at extreme left.

Muhammed Ali accepts a 1971 plate.

British Prime Minister Thatcher accepts a Goebel owl in 1982.

Vice President Rockefeller accepts an eagle from Wilhelm Goebel in 1976.

Former Chancellor Willy Brandt visiting Goebel at a Berlin trade fair in 1956.

Former Federal President Karl Karstens (far left) accepts a Merry Wanderer in January, 1984.

A 1969 ribbon-cutting ceremony at Crestwick-Hummelwerk: Franz Goebel (second from right); Crestwick-Hummelwerk president Morris Kule (far right).

Above: Goebel has become an ambassador of German industry through participation in the German Pavilion at the Walt Disney EPCOT Center in Florida. Here, Dieter Schneider (center) presents an eagle to W. Cardon Walker, who was Chairman of the Board of Walt Disney Productions at the time of this 1982 ceremony. Wilhelm Goebel looks on at right.

Right: The American Bald Eagle from Goebel's Eden Gallery Collection, modeled by Gerhard Skrobek, has been received by dignitaries and celebrities around the world.

Above: Master Sculptor Gerhard Skrobek unveils his seven-foot-high Merry Wanderer for Goebel officials at the opening of the Goebel Collector's Club in 1976, in Tarrytown, New York. Left to right: Günther Neubauer; Dieter Schneider; Wilhelm Goebel; Ulrich Stocke; Joan Ostroff.

Left: Goebel is looking toward the future with the development of new and innovative collector and decorative items. This M.I. Hummel pendant designed by Robert Olszewski is one of a new line of Goebel miniatures available to collectors today.

collectors all across the United States and Canada, and the response has been phenomenal," vice president and executive director Joan Ostroff says. "Gerhard Skrobek's tours have enabled collectors to view his artistry firsthand. And the Facsimile Factory has drawn thousands of visitors everywhere it has appeared. Collectors are eager to see the magic of the hands that make Goebel products. We feel it's important to offer collectors a variety of activities that bring them together so they can feel as though they, too, are part of the Goebel family."

Goebel also embarked on a second major educational effort in 1976 with the publication of the first authorized collector's guide to M.I. Hummel figurines. This book represented one of the first *catalogues raisonnées* ever published on the subject of contemporary collectibles. It is considered the authoritative reference work on M.I. Hummel art and is used not only by collectors and dealers, but by appraisers, auctioneers and insurance companies as well.

"Through the book we were able to tell our story to the collectors so that they could develop a basic understanding of the life of Sister Maria Innocentia Hummel and to catalogue accurately all of the collection," Wilhelm Goebel says. "There were many myths and rumors floating around among collectors. For example, many people thought our factory had been destroyed by a fire. This and other stories were just pure nonsense and the book helped correct all that."

Both the book and the Goebel Collectors' Club have served to broaden the market for M.I. Hummel figurines while helping to direct more attention to the concept of collecting as an important family-oriented leisure-time activity. Festivals in Eaton, Ohio, and Hunter Mountain, New York, drew tens of thousands of visitors over a weekend, and newspapers across the country as well as in Europe suddenly focused attention on the M.I. Hummel collecting phenomenon. Columns about M.I. Hummel collecting started to appear in hobby magazines and leisure sections of Sunday newspapers. A healthy secondary market started to develop with a focus on variations and older figurines.

Perhaps the most important development came about when, in the late 1970's, several of the world's premier auction houses began featuring M.I. Hummel figurines in their sales. Selling of the figurines by these and other regional auctioneers clearly reinforced the secondary market and started a trend of old and hard-to-find pieces being bought up as investments by collectors and non-collectors alike.

The success of the M.I. Hummel art produced by Goebel created a great wave of imitations. Although the quality-minded collector and expert can detect a copy from an original by looking at the details, it has been proven the safest way to be sure a figurine is an authentic M.I. Hummel creation is to look at the bottom for the "M.I. Hummel" mark, and/or one of the traditional Goebel trademarks.

Under the leadership of Wilhelm Goebel, Goebel has become a diversified international company whose M.I. Hummel figurines, dinnerware, and other porcelain and ceramic products are distributed in eighty-eight countries. Goebel was the first German firm to make a commitment to the new Walt Disney EPCOT Center in Orlando, Florida. The Goebel exhibition focuses on contemporary collecting, with particular emphasis on collecting as a family activity. Half a century after the golden alliance between Franz Goebel and Sister Maria Innocentia Hummel began, the spirit of that relationship is helping to move the world of collecting into the twenty-first century.

Left: From time to time, Goebel has manufactured M.I. Hummel dolls in authentic Bavarian costumes. These dolls are treasured by collectors, especially at a time when doll collecting is rapidly becoming a major international hobby.

Below, left to right:
Stormy Weather, HUM 71. Many
size variations. First modeled
by Unger in 1937.

March Winds, HUM 43. Older
pieces slightly larger. Many size
variations.

The M.I. Hummel Gallery represents a major departure from the structured formats that are the focal points of many art books and collectors' guides. This refreshing new approach offers the opportunity to look at M.I. Hummel figurines not simply as catalogued objects but in active displays that help capture the true spirit of Sister Maria Innocentia Hummel's art.

Professor Dr. Ulrich Gertz, a noted German art historian and specialist in porcelain, ceramics and sculpture, says: "We can look at the faces of Sister Maria Innocentia's children...as a mixture of reality and the ideal. They have a particular animation that makes them come alive in the mind of the most casual observer and create sparks of emotion." (See Chapter Five for more of Professor Dr. Gertz's comments.) This same mixture of the real and the ideal, this animation, has been translated to the figurines and now, in this Gallery, the figurines come alive as though they were indeed the children drawn by Sister Maria Innocentia.

Book designer Massimo Vignelli and photographer Walter Pfeiffer have striven to develop innovative themes that create an atmosphere much akin to displaying figurines in one's own home. And the impeccable color reproduction of the collection allows the nuances of the muted colors often used by Sister Maria Innocentia in her original art, as well as the bright tones she sometimes emphasized, to speak for themselves.

The collection reveals, in three-dimensional form, many of the themes that Sister Maria Innocentia incorporated into her drawings. Most prominent among these are the bright-eyed children in traditional German folk dress. Capturing their playful, innocent spirit gave the artist great pleasure for, having spent her own childhood in Bavaria, she had been just such a child herself.

In some instances, Sister Maria Innocentia is known to have created drawings of the local townspeople of Saulgau, just about a mile from the Siessen Convent. A famous example, HUM 154, *Waiter,* is a figurine based on such a drawing—that of a young man who worked as a waiter at the Kleber-Post Hotel during Sister Maria Innocentia's years at Siessen. Visitors to the hotel can still see a drawing of the young waiter done by the artist. Most of the themes, however, represent a synthesis of Sister Maria Innocentia's own childhood visions and experiences and her religious perspective.

This collection was developed from official Goebel records. It includes new photography of all M.I. Hummel figurines that have been authorized by the Siessen Convent for production to date, and that have been released by Goebel.

All the information contained in the captions of this chapter is based upon the research of co-author/authority Robert L. Miller. Frequently, reference is made to the year in which the figurine was first modeled, by whom, and other pertinent facts of interest to serious collectors. These include color, size and modeling variations, as well as reference to older figurines, as denoted by the trademark appearing on the base of each one. A section offering detailed information on the trademarks and when they were used can be found in the appendix on page 304.

A chapter discussing further information of interest to advanced and specialized collectors, written by Robert L. Miller, begins on page 260. Readers can also cross-reference figurines in this chapter through the index, which begins on page 308.

Below, left to right:
Umbrella Girl, HUM 152 B.
*Modeled by Möller in 1949. Many
size variations. Crown mark
extremely rare.*

Umbrella Boy, HUM 152 A. *Crown
mark very rare.*

Below, left to right.
Globe Trotter, HUM 79. Modeled
by Möller in 1937. Remodeled
in 1955. New model has single
weave in basket. Some older
models have green hat.

Happy Traveler, HUM 109.
Produced in all trademarks.
Restyled in 1980 with new
textured finish.

Merry Wanderer, HUM 7. First modeled by Möller in 1935. Can be found in more size variations than any other figurine. Some older models feature "stairstep" base. Restyled in 1972 with new textured finish.

Below, left to right:

Bashful, HUM 377. *First released in United States in 1972.*

Soldier Boy, HUM 332. *First released in United States in 1963. Newer pieces have blue hat ornament; older pieces have red.*

Little Drummer, HUM 240. *First modeled by Unger in 1955.*

Volunteers, HUM 50. *First modeled by Unger in 1936.*

Surprise, HUM 94. *Older pieces have rectangular base. Newer pieces have oval base. First modeled in 1938.*

We Congratulate, HUM 220. *First modeled by Möller in 1952.*

Brother, HUM 95. *Many size and color variations. First modeled in 1938.*

Which Hand? HUM 258. *First modeled in 1962. First appeared in United States in 1964.*

Opposite page, top, left to right:
Wayside Harmony, HUM 111;
Crossroads, HUM 331; Little Hiker,
HUM 16; Home From Market,
HUM 198.

Opposite page, bottom, left to right:
School Boy, HUM 82; Off To
School, HUM 329; Going To
Grandma's, HUM 52.

Top:
Smiling Through, HUM 408.
*Exclusive special edition for
Goebel Collectors' Club members
for 1985.*

Above, left to right:
Mountaineer, HUM 315; Farewell,
HUM 65; Little Cellist, HUM 89; The
Run-A-Way, HUM 327.

The Run-A-Way, HUM 327. Older trademarks considered rare.

Little Cellist, HUM 89. Modeled by Möller in 1938. Restyled in 1960's.

Strolling Along, HUM 5. First modeled by Möller in 1935. Color of dog will vary.

Auf Wiedersehen, HUM 153. Restyled in recent years. Variation with boy wearing hat considered very rare.

Top, left to right:
Good Luck! HUM 419 *(rear view)*.
Good Luck! HUM 419. *Modeled by Skrobek in 1981. Possible future edition.*
Pleasant Journey, HUM 406. *Modeled by Skrobek in 1974. Possible future edition.*

Above, left to right:
Lucky Boy, HUM 335. *Modeled by Möller in 1956. Possible future edition.*
Flower Vendor, HUM 381. *First introduced in United States in 1972.*

Visiting An Invalid, HUM 382.
Modeled by Skrobek and
introduced in United States in
1972.

Going Home, HUM 383. Modeled
by Skrobek in 1966. To be released
in United States in 1985.

Below, left to right:
Hear Ye, Hear Ye, HUM 15.
Modeled by Möller in 1935. Some variation in color of mittens. To be released in United States in 1985.

The Mail Is Here, HUM 226.
Modeled by Möller in 1952.

Opposite page:
Meditation, HUM 13. *Modeled by*
Unger in 1935. Restyled in 1978
by Skrobek. New model has no
flowers in basket. Some older
models have variation in size of
pigtail and hair ribbon.

Above, left to right:
Latest News, HUM 184. *Modeled*
by Möller in 1946. Restyled in
mid-1960's. Old models have
square base. New models have
round base.
Postman, HUM 119. *Modeled by*
Möller in 1939. Restyled by Skrobek
in 1970 with textured finish. Many
size variations.

Top, left to right:
To Market, HUM 49. *First modeled by Möller in 1936. Some early marks considered rare in 6½-inch size.*
Follow the Leader, HUM 369. *Modeled by Skrobek in 1964. Released in United States in 1972.*

Above, left to right:
What Now? HUM 422. *Special 1983-84 edition for members of Goebel Collectors' Club.*
Coffee Break, HUM 409. *Special 1984-85 edition for Goebel Collectors' Club members.*
Valentine Gift, HUM 387. *Special edition #1 for members of Goebel Collectors' Club in 1977.*
Valentine Joy, HUM 399. *Closed edition. Introduced for members of Goebel Collectors' Club in 1980. These four figurines will not be sold as open editions.*

Below, left to right:
It's Cold, HUM 421. *Special 1982*
Collectors' Club edition #6.

Daisies Don't Tell, HUM 380.
Collectors' Club edition #5 for
1981.

Below, left to right:
Happy Pastime, HUM 69; I Won't
Hurt You, HUM 428; Friend or Foe,
HUM 434. HUM 428 *and* HUM 434
are possible future editions.

True Friendship, HUM 402.
Modeled by Skrobek in 1973.
Possible future edition.

Top, left to right:
Honey Lover, HUM 312. *First modeled in 1955. Possible future edition.*
Being Punished, *Wall Plaque,* HUM 326. *Modeled in 1957 by Skrobek. Possible future edition.*

Above, left to right:
The Florist, HUM 349. *Modeled by Skrobek in 1957. Possible future edition.*
Honey Lover, HUM 312. *Possible future edition.*

Top, left to right:
Max and Moritz, HUM 123.
Modeled by Möller in 1939.
Restyled in early 1970's with new
textured finish.
Congratulations, HUM 17. *First*
modeled in 1935 by Unger. Older
models do not have socks. Restyled
by Skrobek in 1971 with new
textured finish. Old 7¾-inch to
8¼-inch pieces very rare.

Above, left to right:
Smart Little Sister, HUM 346;
Carnival, HUM 328; Star Gazer,
HUM 132.

Opposite page, left to right:
Gay Adventure, HUM 356.
Modeled by Skrobek in 1963.
Released in United States in 1972.
Trumpet Boy, HUM 97. *Modeled*
by Möller in 1938. Many size
variations. "U.S. Zone" mark piece
has blue coat shaded with green.
Boy's coat is normally green.

Below, left to right.
Out of Danger, HUM 56B.
Modeled by Möller in 1952.
Variation in height and size of
base.

Culprits, HUM 56A. Modeled by
Möller in 1936. Restyled in later
years. Restyled pieces have extra
branch by boy's feet.

Apple Tree Boy, HUM 142.
Modeled by Möller in 1940.
Restyled many times over the
years. Many size variations.
Smaller models made without bird
in tree.

Apple Tree Girl, HUM 141. Modeled
by Möller in 1940. Restyled many
times over the years. Many size
variations. Smaller models made
without bird in tree.

Where Did You Get That? HUM 417. *Possible future edition.*

Do I Dare? HUM 411. *Modeled by Skrobek in 1978. Possible future edition.*

An Apple A Day, HUM 403.
Modeled by Skrobek in 1973.
Possible future edition.

Whistler's Duet, HUM 413.
Modeled by Skrobek in 1979.
Possible future edition.

Well Done! HUM 400. *Modeled by*
Skrobek in 1973. Possible future
edition.

Top, left to right:
At The Fence, HUM 324. *Modeled by Möller in 1956. Possible future edition.*
Behave! HUM 339. *Modeled in 1956. Possible future edition.*
Not For You! HUM 317. *Introduced in the United States in 1961.*

Above, left to right:
Coquettes, HUM 179. *Modeled by Möller in 1946.*
At The Fence, HUM 324. *Modeled by Möller in 1955.*
Feathered Friends, HUM 344. *Full bee and stylized pieces considered rare.*

Opposite page, left to right:
Singing Lesson, HUM 63. *Modeled by Möller in 1937. Slight variation in tilt of boy's head and position of hand.*
Timid Little Sister, HUM 394. *First released in United States in 1981.*

She Loves Me, She Loves Me Not!
HUM 174. *Modeled by Möller in 1945. Restyled several times.*

Sensitive Hunter, HUM 6; *Friends,* HUM 136; *Good Hunting!* HUM 307; *Retreat to Safety,* HUM 201.

Mischief Maker, HUM 342; *Just Resting,* HUM 112; *Chicken-Licken!* HUM 385.

Book Ends: Little Goat Herder, HUM 250A; *Feeding Time,* HUM 250B; *Apple Tree Girl,* HUM 252A; *Apple Tree Boy,* HUM 252B.

Shepherd's Boy, HUM 64; *Lost Sheep*, HUM 68; *Good Friends*, HUM 182; *Little Goat Herder*, HUM 200; *Favorite Pet*, HUM 361; *Just Resting*, HUM 112.

Barnyard Hero, HUM 195; *Goose Girl*, HUM 47; *Be Patient*, HUM 197; *Playmates*, HUM 58; *Easter Time*, HUM 384; *Farm Boy*, HUM 66.

Don't Be Shy, HUM 379; *Companions*, HUM 370; *Daddy's Girls*, HUM 371; *Just Fishing*, HUM 373; *The Botanist*, HUM 351; *Lute Song*, HUM 368.

Top, left to right:
Chick Girl, HUM 57. Modeled by
Unger in 1936. Remodeled by
Skrobek in 1964. Variations in
design of base.
Feeding Time, HUM 199. Modeled
in 1948 by Möller, with blonde
hair. Restyled in 1960's by
Skrobek. Girl has dark hair and
new facial features.

Above, left to right:
Sister, HUM 98; Easter Greetings,
HUM 378; Little Shopper, HUM 96.

Opposite page:
Cinderella, HUM 337. First
introduced in United States in
1972. Modeled by Möller in 1956.
Restyled by Skrobek in 1972.
Older models with open eyes
considered rare.

Top left to right:
Playmates, *Book End,* HUM 61A;
Chick Girl, *Book End,* HUM 61B.
*First produced in 1936. Trademarks
stamped on wood base rather
than on figurine. Crown mark
considered rare.*

Above, left to right:
Goose Girl, *Book End,* HUM 60B.
*First produced in 1936. Trademarks
stamped on wood base. Crown
mark considered rare.*
Farm Boy, *Book End,* HUM 60A.

Top, left to right:
Good Friends, *Book End,* HUM 251A. *Designed in 1960. Appeared in United States in 1964.*
She Loves Me, She Loves Me Not!, *Book End,* HUM 251B.

Above, left to right:
Sing With Me, HUM 405. *Modeled by Skrobek in 1973. To be released in United States in 1985.*
Forty Winks, HUM 401. *Possible future edition.*
Flute Song, HUM 407. *Possible future edition.*
Spring Bouquet, HUM 398. *Possible future edition.*

*In Tune, HUM 414. Modeled by
Skrobek in 1979. Released in
United States in 1981.*

Opposite page, left to right:
What's New? HUM 418. *Modeled by Skrobek in 1980. Possible future edition.*
The Poet, HUM 397. *Modeled by Skrobek in 1973. Possible future edition.*

Above, left to right:
Book Worm, HUM 3. *Modeled by Möller in 1935. Restyled by Skrobek in 1972. Larger pieces have two flowers on page.*
Thoughtful, HUM 415. *Modeled by Skrobek in 1979. First released in United States in 1981.*
Book Worm, HUM 3 *(rear view).*
Busy Student, HUM 367. *First released in United States in 1964.*
Mother's Helper, HUM 133. *Modeled in 1939 by Möller. This is the only figurine in current production with a cat.*

Below, left to right:
Book Worm, HUM 3. Book Worm,
Book End, Boy, HUM 14A. Book
Worm, *Book End, Girl,* HUM 14B.
Book Worm, *Book End, Girl,* HUM
14B *(rear view).*

Top, left to right:
Little Scholar, HUM 80.
Arithmetic Lesson, HUM 303.
Possible future edition.
School Girl, HUM 81.
School Girl, HUM 81 *(larger version).*

Above, left to right:
The Professor, HUM 320. *Modeled by Skrobek in 1955. Possible future edition.*
School Boy, HUM 82. *Modeled by Möller in 1938. Many size variations. Large size crown mark considered rare.*

Below, left to right:
Is It Raining? HUM 420. *Modeled by Skrobek in 1981. Possible future edition.*

Truant, HUM 410. *Modeled by Skrobek in 1978. Possible future edition.*

Below, left to right:
Truant, HUM 410.

Bath Time, HUM 412. *First modeled by Skrobek in 1978. Possible future edition.*

Pleasant Journey, HUM 406. First
modeled by Skrobek in 1974.
Possible future edition.

Above, left to right:
Chimney Sweep, HUM 12 (rear view). Modeled by Möller in 1935. Restyled several times over the years.
Chimney Sweep, HUM 12.
Mother's Darling, HUM 175. Modeled by Möller in 1945. Restyled several times. Older models have pink and green kerchiefs. Newer models have blue ones.

Top, left to right:
The Builder, HUM 305. Modeled by Skrobek in 1955. Introduced in United States in 1963. Full bee mark considered very rare.
Little Thrifty, Bank, HUM 118. Modeled by Möller in 1939. Restyled in 1963.

Opposite page:
Wash Day, HUM 321. *Modeled in 1955. Introduced in United States in 1963. Full bee mark rare.*

Below, left to right:
Sister, HUM 98; Little Shopper, HUM 96; On Holiday, HUM 350; Sweet Greetings, HUM 352; Little Sweeper, HUM 171.

Bottom:
Big Housecleaning, HUM 363. *First modeled by Skrobek in 1959. Introduced in United States in 1972.*

Below, left to right:
Happy Birthday, HUM 176.
Modeled by Möller in 1945.
Restyled in 1979 with oval base.
Old model had round base.

Going to Grandma's, HUM 52.
Modeled in 1936 by Unger.

Objects inside cone represent
candy and sweets, not flowers.
Cone appears empty on large
models. Restyled in 1960's and in
1979. Crown marks considered
rare.

*Begging His Share, HUM 9.
Modeled by Möller in 1935. Many
size variations. Restyled in 1964
without hole for candle in cake.
Old models have brightly colored
striped socks.*

Opposte page:
For Father, HUM 87. *Modeled by*
Möller in 1938. Some old models
have carrot-colored vegetables.
Most pieces have boy holding
white radishes.

Above, left to right:
Boots, HUM 143. *First modeled by*
Möller in 1940. Restyled in late
1970's by Skrobek with textured
finish. Many size variations.
Boots, HUM 143 *(rear view).*
Weary Wanderer, HUM 204.
Modeled by Unger in 1949. Word
"Lauterbach" on back of figurine is
the name of a village used in an
old German song. Restyled with
textured finish.
Lost Stocking, HUM 374. *Modeled*
by Skrobek in 1965. Released in
United States in 1972.

Below, left to right:
Baker, HUM 128. *Modeled by Möller in 1939. Restyled several times, most recently in the mid-1970's with textured finish.*

Hello, HUM 124. *Many size variations. Many color variations in coat, trousers and vest. Crown marks are considered rare.*

Waiter, HUM 154. *First produced with gray coat and gray-striped trousers. Now has blue coat and tan-striped trousers. Various names used on bottle, most prominent being "Rhein Wine." Crown mark considered rare.*

Rhein-Wine

angle view).

Little Bookkeeper, HUM 306.
Modeled in 1955 by Möller.
Introduced in United States in
1962. Full bee mark considered
rare.

A Fair Measure, HUM 345. *Full bee*
mark considered rare.

Below, left to right.
Little Pharmacist, HUM 322.
*Introduced in United States in
1962. Variations on bottle name,
mostly "Rizinusöl," or "Vitamins."
Full bee mark rare.*

Boy With Toothache, HUM 217.
Modeled by Möller in 1951.

Below, left to right:
Little Nurse, HUM 376. *Released in
United States in 1982.*

Doctor, HUM 127. *Modeled by
Möller in 1939. Has been restyled
with textured finish.*

Above, left to right:
An Emergency, HUM 436; Pleasant
Moment, HUM 425; Sing Along,
HUM 433.

Opposite page:
Spring Cheer, HUM 72. *Modeled
by Unger in 1937. Restyled in 1965
by Skrobek. Older models with
dark green dress considered rare.*
Confidentially, HUM 314. *Modeled
in 1955. Introduced in United
States in 1972. Full bee mark
considered rare.*
Little Gardener, HUM 74. *Modeled
by Unger in 1937. Many color
variations.*

Below, left to right.
Sunny Morning, HUM 313.
Modeled by Möller in 1955.
Possible future edition.

I Forgot, HUM 362. *Possible future*
edition.

Relaxation, HUM 316. *Possible*
future edition.

Morning Stroll, HUM 375.
Modeled by Skrobek in 1964.
Possible future edition.

Below, left to right:
Sleep Tight, HUM 424; Delicious,
HUM 435.

Below, left to right:
Girl With Doll, HUM 239B.
Boy With Horse, HUM 239C.
Prayer Before Battle, HUM 20.
Modeled in 1935 by Möller.
Girl With Nosegay, HUM 239A.

Bottom:
Horse Trainer, HUM 423.

Below, left to right:
Doll Mother, HUM 67; Blessed Event, HUM 333; Stitch In Time, HUM 255; Happy Pastime, HUM 69; Little Tailor, HUM 308; Knitting Lesson, HUM 256; Doll Bath, HUM 319; Kiss Me, HUM 311.

Below, left to right:
The Tuba Player, HUM 437; In
D-Major, HUM 430. *Both are
possible future editions.*

Above, left to right:
Sad Song, HUM 404. *First modeled
by Skrobek in 1973. Possible
future edition.*
HUM 447. *English name is still
open for this figurine. Possible
future edition.*

Below, left to right:
Soloist, HUM 135. Modeled by Möller in 1940. Many size variations.

Duet, HUM 130. Modeled by Möller in 1939. Early crown mark pieces have small "lip" on edge of base.

Street Singer, HUM 131. Modeled by Möller in 1939. Many size and color variations.

Serenade, HUM 85. Modeled by Möller in 1938. Recently restyled with textured finish. Some variations in color of hat. Crown marks considered rare.

Band Leader, HUM 129. Modeled by Möller in 1939.

Duet, HUM 130 (rear view).

Below, left to right:
Let's Sing, HUM 110. *Modeled by Unger in 1938.*

Joyful, HUM 53. *Modeled by Unger in 1936. Some early crown mark pieces have orange dress and blue shoes, considered rare. Current models have a brown-colored mandolin.*

Close Harmony, HUM 336.

Birthday Serenade, HUM 218. *Modeled by Unger in 1952. Remodeled in 1964 by Skrobek.*

Happiness, HUM 86. Modeled
by Unger in 1938. Many size
variations.

Girl With Accordian, HUM 259.
*Closed number. First modeled in
1962. Never released into current
production program. Only samples
exist.*

Girl With Sheet of Music, HUM
389. *Modeled by Skrobek in 1968.*

Birthday Serenade, HUM 218.

Boy With Accordian, HUM 390.
Modeled by Skrobek in 1968.

Girl With Trumpet, HUM 391.
Modeled by Skrobek in 1968.

Above, left to right:
Puppy Love, HUM 1. *First modeled by Möller in 1935.*
Little Fiddler, HUM 4.
Little Cellist, HUM 89. *Modeled by Möller in 1938. Restyled in 1960's. Older pieces have rectangular base while newer pieces have corners squared off.*

Opposite page:
Sweet Music, HUM 186. *Modeled by Unger in 1947. Crown mark pieces with white slippers with blue-green stripes considered rare.*

Little Fiddler, HUM 2. *Modeled by Möller in 1935. Large crown mark and full bee pieces considered rare.*

Ring Around the Rosie, HUM 348.
Modeled by Skrobek in 1957.
Full bee pieces very rare. Stylized
pieces also rare.

Below, left to right.
Happy Days, HUM 150.

Spring Dance, HUM 353.
*Introduced in United States in
1964.*

Follow the Leader, HUM 369.
*Modeled by Skrobek in 1964.
Released in United States in 1972.*

Opposite page, left to right,
Table Lamps:
Culprits, HUM 44A; Birthday
Serenade, HUM 234; Happy Days,
HUM 232; Apple Tree Girl, HUM
229; She Loves Me, She Loves Me
Not! HUM 227.

This page, left to right:
To Market, *Table Lamp,* HUM 223;
Little Band, *Candle Holder on
Music Box,* HUM 388M.

Above, left to right:
Skier, HUM 59. *Modeled by Unger in 1936. Older models had wooden poles. Newer models have metal poles. Some models have appeared with plastic poles.*
Letter to Santa Claus, HUM 340. *Modeled in 1956. First introduced in United States in 1971. Completely restyled by Skrobek in 1970.*

Opposite page:
Ride Into Christmas, HUM 396. *Modeled by Skrobek in 1970. Introduced in United States in 1972.*

Below, left to right:
With Loving Greetings, HUM 309.
Released in United States in 1983.

Birthday Present, HUM 341.
Possible future edition.

Knit One, Purl One, HUM 432.
Modeled by Skrobek in 1982.

Helping Mother, HUM 325. *Possible
future edition.*

Birthday Cake, HUM 338. *Possible future edition.*

Concentration, HUM 302. *Possible future edition.*

Baking Day, HUM 330. *To be released in the United States in 1985.*

Little Helper, HUM 73. *Modeled in 1937 by Unger.*

Top, left to right:
Girl With Nosegay, *Advent Candlestick,* HUM 115; Angel With Accordion, HUM 238B; Boy With Horse, *Advent Candlestick,* HUM 117; Angle With Lute, HUM 238A; Heavenly Lullaby, HUM 262; Angelic Song, HUM 144; Girl With Fir Tree, *Advent Candlestick,* HUM 116; Angel With Trumpet, HUM 238C.

Above left to right:
Christmas Song, HUM 343; Watchful Angel, HUM 194; Littlest Angel, HUM 365; Christmas Angel, HUM 301.

Opposite page:
Lamb From Nativity Set , HUM 214/0; Angel Serenade, HUM 260/E; Blessed Child, HUM 78.

Below, left to right:
Tuneful Angel, HUM 359; Bird Duet,
HUM 169; Flying Angel, HUM 366;
Silent Night, *Candle Holder,* HUM
54; Shining Light, HUM 358; Little
Guardian, HUM 145; Whitsuntide,
HUM 163; Guiding Angel, HUM
357.

Opposite page:
Angel Lights, *Candleholder,*
HUM 241.

Below, left to right:
Joyous News, HUM 27; Festival
Harmony *(flute),* HUM 173;
Festival Harmony *(mandolin),*
HUM 172; Christ Child, HUM 18;
Candlelight, *Candleholder,* HUM
192; Celestial Musician, HUM 188;
Heavenly Angel, HUM 21.

Top, left to right:
English name for this figurine is still
open, HUM 438; A Gentle Glow,
HUM 439; HUM 438. *Both are*
possible future editions.

Above, left to right:
Angel Duet, *Candle Holder,* HUM
193; Angelic Sleep, *Candle Holder,*
HUM 25; Little Gabriel, HUM 32.

Opposite page, left to right:
Birthday Candle, HUM 440.
Possible future edition.
Well Done! HUM 400. *Possible*
future edition.

Nativity Set with Wooden Stable,
HUM 214.
Flying Angel, HUM 366.
*This nativity set was modeled by
Unger in 1951, and first produced
and sold in 1952. It is also
available in individual pieces.*

At one time this set was produced
and sold in white overglaze finish,
but it is no longer sold this way.
The white overglaze finish is
considered rare. Early production
of HUM 214A (Virgin Mary and
Infant Jesus) was made in one
piece. Because of production
problems, it was later produced
as two separate pieces, both with
the same number (214A) incised in
the bottom of each piece. Two
different styles of lambs (214/0) have
been used with the Nativity sets.

Some Nativity set pieces have an
incised 1951 copyright date.
Wooden stable is usually sold
separately. The sixteenth piece,
Flying Angel, HUM 366, was added
to the set in 1963.

Large Nativity Set With Wooden Stable, HUM 260. *Modeled in 1968 by Skrobek. Various types of wooden stables have been used over the years.*

Above:
Flower Madonna, HUM 10.
Rare in this color.

Opposite page:
Supreme Protection, HUM 364.
*First released in 1984 in honor of
75th anniversary of Sister Maria
Innocentia Hummel's birth.
Production limited to 1984.*

Below, left to right:
Madonna Holding Child, HUM 151.
*Modeled by Unger in 1942. Many
color variations. Crown and full
bee marks rare.*
Flower Madonna, HUM 10.
*Modeled by Unger in 1935. Halo
modified from open flat style in
mid-1950's. Many color variations.*

Bottom, left to right:
Madonna Without Halo, HUM 46.
Blessed Mother, HUM 372.
Possible future edition.
Madonna With Halo, HUM 45.

Saint George, HUM 55.

Top, left to right: Children's Prayer, HUM 448; Pay Attention, HUM 426; Hello World, HUM 429; The Surprise, HUM 431; Where Are You? HUM 427.

Above, left to right:
On Secret Path, HUM 386; Bird Watcher, HUM 300; Forest Shrine, HUM 183; Eventide, HUM 99; On Secret Path, HUM 386 *(rear view)*.

Opposite page, left to right:
Village Boy, HUM 51; For Mother, HUM 257 *(new smaller size)*; Girl With Nosegay, HUM 239A; Worship, HUM 84; For Mother, HUM 257.

Top, left to right,
Holy Water Fonts:
Angel Facing Right, HUM 91 B;
White Angel, HUM 75; Dove, HUM
393; Angel Facing Left, HUM 91 A.

Center, top row, left to right,
Holy Water Fonts:
The Good Shepherd, HUM 35;
Child Jesus, HUM 26; Guardian
Angel, HUM 248.
Center, bottom row, left to right,
Holy Water Fonts:
Heavenly Angel, HUM 207; Angel
Shrine, HUM 147; Angel Duet,
HUM 146; Worship, HUM 164.

Bottom, top row, left to right,
Holy Water Fonts:
Angel With Birds, HUM 22;
Madonna And Child, HUM 243;
Holy Family, HUM 246.
Bottom, bottom row, left to right,
Holy Water Fonts:
Child With Flowers, HUM 36;
Angel With Bird, HUM 167; Angel
Cloud, HUM 206.

Opposite page:
Madonna Plaque, HUM 48.
Modeled by Unger in 1936.

158

Opposite page, left to right:
Searching Angel, *Wall Plaque,*
HUM 310; Merry Christmas, *Wall
Plaque,* HUM 323.

Below:
Tuneful Good Night, *Wall Plaque,*
HUM 180.

Above left:
Flitting Butterfly, *Wall Plaque,* HUM 139. *Modeled by Möller in 1940. Some design and color variations.*

Center, left to right:
Ba-Bee Ring, HUM 30A; Ba-Bee Ring, HUM 30B. *Rings modeled in 1935 by Unger. Large version crown mark rare. Crown mark with red ring extremely rare.*

Below left:
Child in Bed, *Wall Plaque,* HUM 137.

Opposite page:
Swaying Lullaby, *Wall Plaque,* HUM 165.

Er träumt von besseren Zeiten

Top, left to right,
Wall Plaques:
Merry Wanderer, HUM 92; Little
Fiddler, HUM 93; Retreat to Safety,
HUM 126.

Above, clockwise from top left,
Wall Plaques:
Quartet, HUM 134; Standing Boy,
HUM 168; Vacation Time, HUM
125; The Mail Is Here, HUM 140.

Right: top to bottom,
Anniversary Plates:
Stormy Weather, *1975,* HUM 280;
Auf Wiedersehn, *1985,* HUM 282;
Ring Around the Rosie, *1980,*
HUM 281.

Top, left to right,
Annual Bells:
Let's Sing, *1978,* HUM 700;
Farewell, *1979,* HUM 701; In Tune,
1981, HUM 703; Thoughtful, *1980,*
HUM 702; She Loves Me, *1982,*
HUM 704; Knit One, *1983,* HUM 705.

Above, left to right,
Annual Bells:
Mountaineer, *1984,* HUM 706; Girl
With Sheet of Music, *1985,* HUM
707; Sing Along, *1986,* HUM 708;
With Loving Greetings, *1987,*
HUM 709; Busy Student, *1988,*
HUM 710; Latest News, *1989,* HUM
711; What's New? *1990,* HUM 712.

Overleaf:
Annual Plates.

Annual Plates.
For HUM numbers and names, see
Index, beginning on page 308.

Top, back row, left to right,
Boxes:
Playmates, HUM III/58; Singing
Lesson, HUM III/63; Let's Sing,
HUM III/110.
Top, front row, left to right,
Boxes:
Joyful, HUM III/53; Happy Pastime,
HUM III/69; Chick Girl, HUM III/57.

Above, top row, left to right,
Ash Trays:
Singing Lesson, HUM 34; Boy With
Bird, HUM 166.
Above, bottom row, left to right,
Ash Trays:
Let's Sing, HUM 114; Happy
Pastime, HUM 62; Joyful, HUM 33.

Below, left to right:
Angel Serenade, HUM 83. *Modeled by Unger in 1938.*

Good Shepherd, HUM 42. *Modeled by Unger in 1935. Large pieces with crown and full bee marks very rare.*

Lullaby, *Candle Holder,* HUM 24.

Angel Duet, *Candleholder,* HUM 193.

Call To Worship, *Clock,* HUM 441.

Above, left to right:
On Holiday, HUM 350. *Modeled by Skrobek in 1964. Introduced in United States in 1981.*
Little Hiker, HUM 16. *Modeled by Möller in 1935.*
Chapel Time, *Clock,* HUM 442.
We Congratulate, HUM 220.

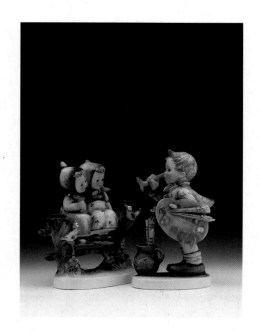

Above, left to right:
Coquettes, HUM 179; The Artist,
HUM 304.

Below, left to right:
Art Critic, HUM 318. *Possible future edition.*
Signs of Spring, HUM 203.

Below, left to right:
Photographer, HUM 178. *Modeled by Unger in 1948. Has been restyled several times.*

Telling Her Secret, HUM 196. *Modeled by Unger in 1948.*

In this day and age, when computerized automation and robotics are making rapid breakthroughs in mass production of consumer goods and industrial products, the idea of goods made by hand almost seems to be a thing of the past—a throwback to a time when human eyes and hands set the standards for quality and excellence. M.I. Hummel figurines are just that—a throwback to the time when true craftsmanship reigned. This is an important reason for their widespread appeal.

At Goebel there is a saying: "Hands make Goebel." M.I. Hummel figurines, made by Goebel, are a true testimonial to the craftsman's art. A work force of 1,500 operates as a team at the Goebel factory in Rödental, near Coburg, producing M.I. Hummel figurines, plates and other collector items. These craftsmen follow the three-century-old tradition of German porcelain and ceramic making.

The road to becoming a full-fledged porcelain craftsman is a three-year apprenticeship. The multi-faceted curriculum includes: technical training at the Bavarian School for Porcelain at Selb; in-house training at the Goebel painting school; and on-the-job training in all phases of production of M.I. Hummel figurines and other Goebel products. Then, and only then, can an apprentice graduate to the proud title of *porzelliner*, the industry classification for a journeyman craftsman.

There are over seven hundred painstaking hand operations involved in the making of a M.I. Hummel figurine at Goebel. In addition, there are fifty quality control checkpoints and inspections to insure that the pieces meet Goebel's high standard of quality. Teamwork and an outstanding work atmosphere make quality the work of the day.

The tradition of the *porzelliner* carries on with the Goebel family as well. In his time, Franz Goebel studied at the State School for Porcelain and Ceramics before going to work for his father, Max-Louis. Wilhelm Goebel spent his apprenticeship at the Bavarian School for Porcelain in Selb, and at Hutschenreuther, one of Germany's great names in porcelain. He also received a ceramic engineering degree from the *Fachhochschule* in Hoehr-Grenzhausen, one of Europe's most famous ceramic schools.

Master sculptors Arthur Möller and Reinhold Unger, who worked with Franz Goebel at transforming the two-dimensional art of Sister Maria Innocentia Hummel into three-dimensional form and were the first to sculpt the M.I. Hummel figurines, came to work at Goebel in 1911 and 1915, respectively. Möller had been educated at the Arts and Crafts Academy in Dresden and at the Academy for Applied Arts in Munich (the same school that Sister Maria Innocentia eventually attended), while Unger studied at the Fine Art School of Professor Hutschenreuther in Lichte and then worked with the *Kunstanstalt Gaigi* in Munich. They passed on their knowledge of sculpting the M.I. Hummel figurines to Gerhard Skrobek, who joined Goebel in 1951 after studying in Berlin at the *Reimannschule* and in Coburg with the well-known sculptor, Poertzel, who created many porcelain pieces for *W. Goebel Porzellanfabrik*. Skrobek, the master sculptor of the figurines today, now passes on his knowledge and skills to the many young apprentices he teaches at the Goebel school.

The hands-on approach that the Goebel family has advocated for generations stresses both quality and tradition. Many of the craftsmen pictured in this section represent the third and fourth generations of their families employed at Goebel. Their commitment to excellence, reflected in each M.I. Hummel figurine and Goebel product, can be seen on the bottom of each piece—in the Goebel trademark.

Opposite page: The birth of an M.I. Hummel figurine. The hands of Master Sculptor Gerhard Skrobek sculpting the first model of a figurine in clay.

Overleaf: Skrobek in his studio at Goebel modeling HUM 348, Ring Around The Rosie. *The figurines are developed from color reproductions of Sister Maria Innocentia's artwork that have been published as art cards or as illustrations in children's books. The card from which Skrobek is working is at the lower right.*

Second overleaf: Skrobek brings a figurine to life. For more than three decades Skrobek has been the individual most responsible for sculpting the details into the figurines to correspond with Sister Maria Innocentia's published art.

Above: Sculptor Rudi Wittmann details a model of HUM 364, Supreme Protection. *Sister Maria Innocentia's religious art presents a particular challenge to Goebel craftsmen, who help transform these sacred images into three-dimensional forms.*

Left: Master Sculptor Gerhard Bochmann in his studio at Goebel. Bochmann, who learned his craft at Meissen and worked there for several years before coming to Goebel, sculpts wildlife studies, and some figurine lines.

Left: The figurine, now sculpted in clay, is examined by Skrobek and Florian Brechelmacher of the moldmaking department. Because of their detail, the figurines cannot be molded in one piece, so the two men must decide how the model can be cut into pieces for moldmaking purposes. Each piece of the model will then have its own mold made. "Even when I am sculpting I have this in mind," Skrobek says.

Top and above: Brechelmacher cuts Ride Into Christmas into pieces for moldmaking.

Left: After Ride Into Christmas *has been cut, it consists of twelve separate pieces. Even the tiny candle that the boy on the sled holds requires its own mold. Some of the larger figurines require as many as thirty separate molds due to the amount of detail on them.*

Above: An original form being made. Additional clay is applied around the head, on a metal foundation.

Overleaf: Liquid plaster of paris is then poured around a piece of the cut-up figurine model, held in by a plastic sheath. When the plaster dries its image appears on the master mold in relief.

Left to right: A close-up view of the master mold being poured. From this plaster of paris mold, a mother form will be made. But instead of being made of plaster, it will be made from an acrylic resin developed in 1954 by Master Sculptor Gerhard Skrobek and a team of Goebel ceramic experts. Goebel helped revolutionize the porcelain and ceramics industry with the development of this acrylic resin. The acrylic resin put an end to the expansion and loss of detail encountered through the use of plaster of paris mother forms.

Overleaf: The acrylic resin mother
forms can be seen at the center left
of the page; they are cream-
colored. The black clay model at
the lower right is the original clay
model. The grey piece on the clay
model is a spout, which allows the
plaster to reach the inside of the
mold. The actual head of the boy
can be seen at the upper right.

Right: A member of the moldmaking department piles a block and case mold onto a skid. Notice the slit through the center of the mold that forms the "lock" and ensures accuracy when parts of the figurine are being cast. These molds can only be used a limited number of times before losing their detail and must be replaced frequently in order not to lose their detail. With each figurine requiring on the average of fifteen, but sometimes needing as many as thirty, different molds to cast all of its parts, moldmaking is one of the major jobs at the factory.

Above: The actual block and case working molds from which the parts of the figurine are cast. The block and case lock into each other to form the mold.

3X 1	7353	80	||
2	HW4 356 54403	20	|||| ||
X 3	1? % 340 389 60 44350 20 Hase 120		|||| ||||
4	Hase 40 Linser Köpfe		||

Left: The number of plaster of paris working molds gets chalked up on an old-time blackboard just as it did when Franz Goebel made his rounds around the factory.

Above: Coats and aprons on their pegs. The end of a working day.

Overleaf: These twenty-four pieces comprise the set of plaster of paris working molds that cast the twelve parts of Ride Into Christmas. *Each has its own number as well as* HUM 396 *incised on its surface.*

Second overleaf: A caster pours liquid ceramic slip into a working mold to cast a figurine part.

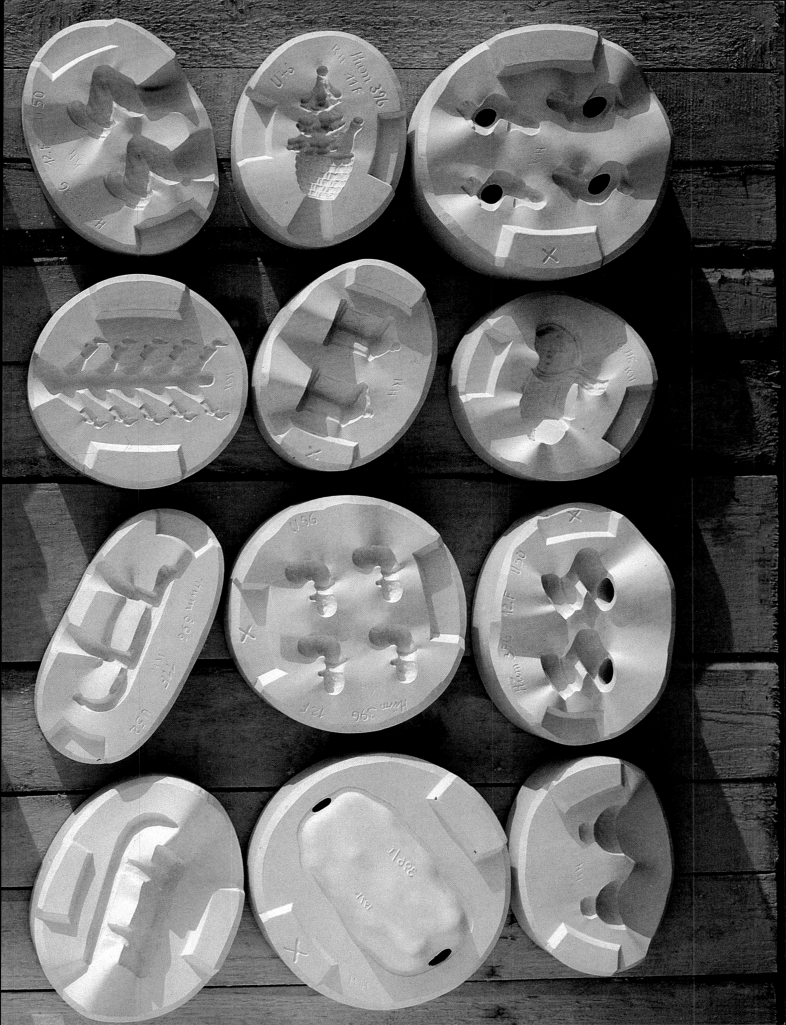

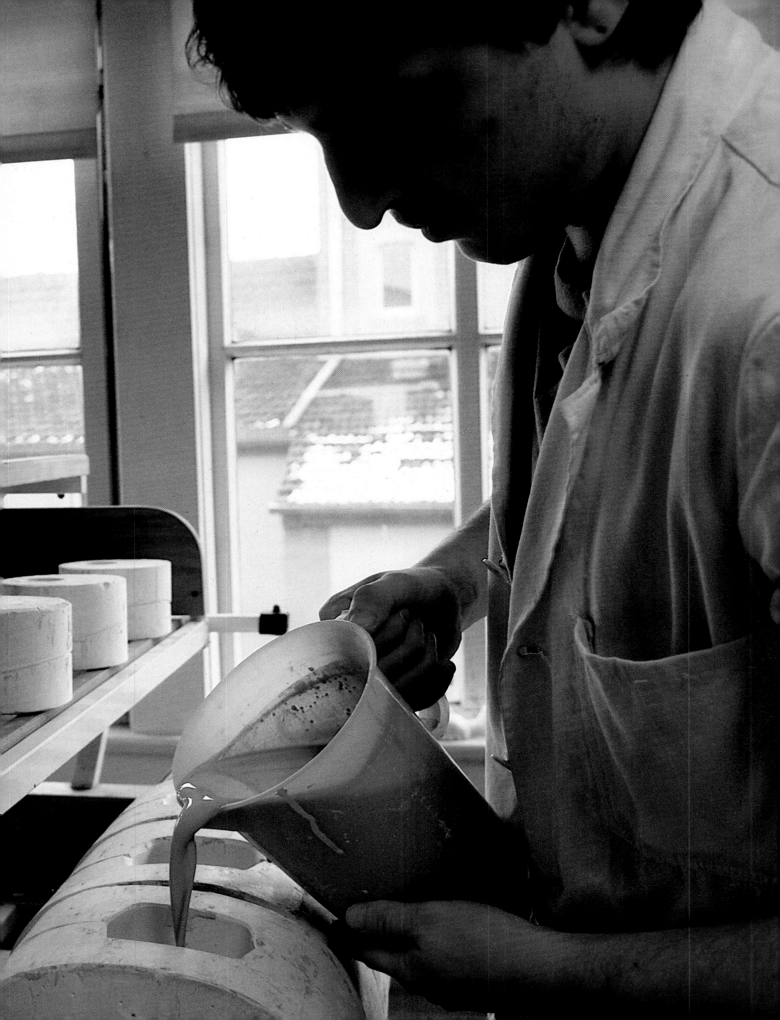

Left to right: A cross-section of the slip as it pours, hardens and dries. This ceramic mass is made from kaolin, feldspar, and quartz, and is designed to withstand the high kiln firing that lets the metallic oxide paints "melt" into the figurine.

The consistency of the formula is monitored frequently by quality control experts in the ceramics lab. The amount of time the slip remains in the mold is timed carefully so that the actual figurine part being cast will dry to a certain thickness.

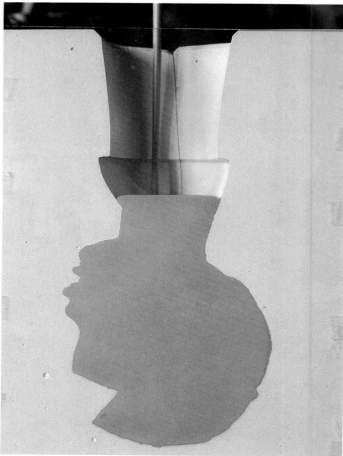

The plaster of paris mold absorbs water from the slip and when the mold is turned, the water and excess slip flow out. This leaves a hollow shell of moist ceramic, which is the cast part.

All figurines are hollow on the inside as the result of this casting process. The cast head is shown in the bottom picture.

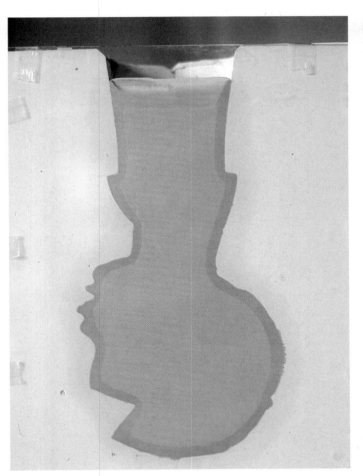

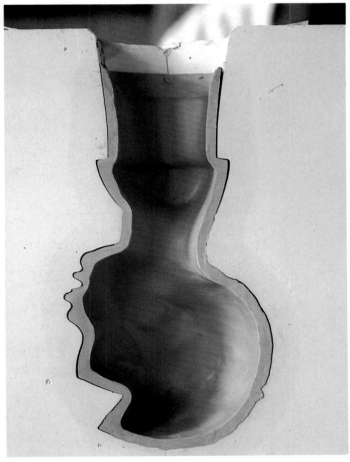

Left and above: Assembly of the figurine from its many pieces is a most delicate craft. Here, HUM 152B, Umbrella Girl *is being put together.*

Overleaf: The assembler carefully places each piece in its proper place using liquid slip to "glue" the joints so as to eliminate the seams. Here, a doll head is getting her front curls.

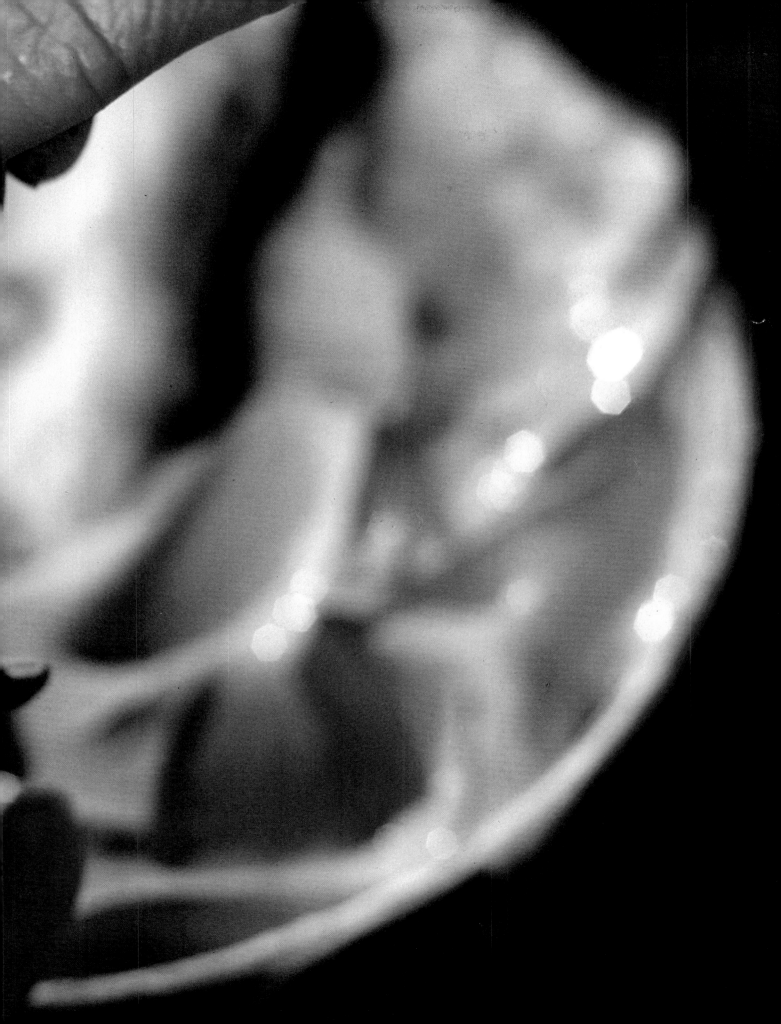

Above and right: The assembler's craft includes detailing the nuances and fine points. These details, which may seem minor when observing the raw ceramic piece here, come to life with painting and firing.

Overleaf: A magnifying glass is used by an assembler to detail HUM 4, Little Fiddler.

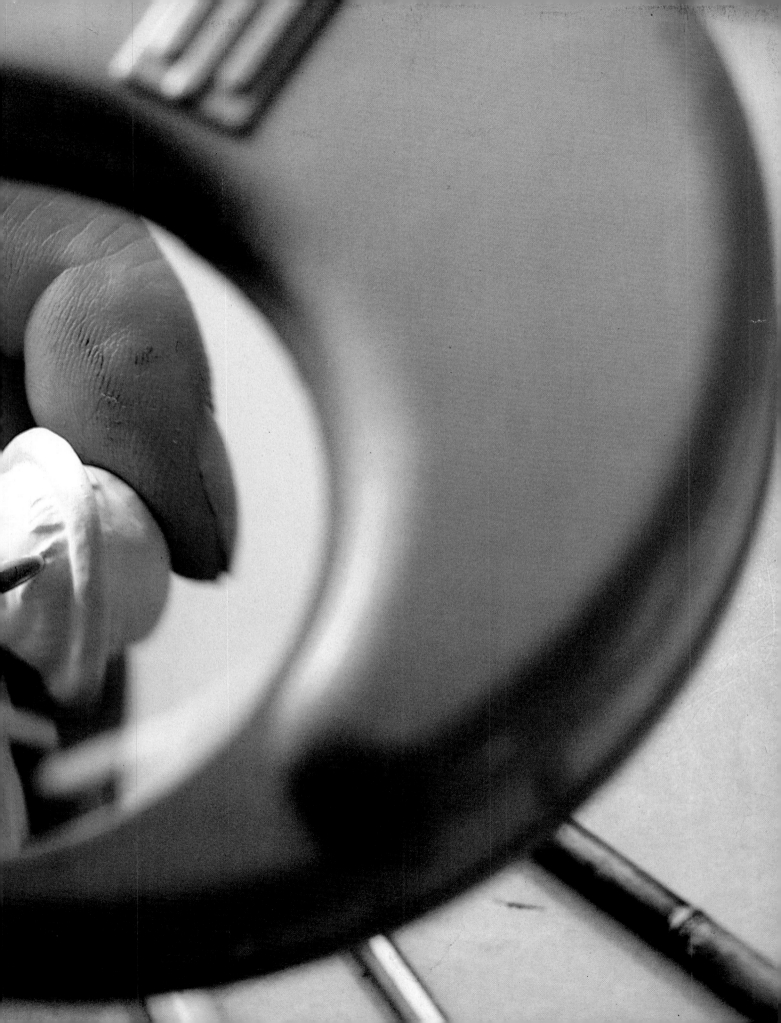

Left and above: The kiln. Here is where tradition and high technology meet. After the assembled figurine is dried in open air it receives its first (bisque) firing at 1140 degrees (celsius) in this state-of-the-art electric kiln. Electricity is used for precise temperature control as well as environmental reasons. After the firing, the pieces remain in the oven for several hours to cool down.

Overleaf: The glazing process requires patience and a good eye. Each piece is hand dipped, reducing the possibility of chipping or breakage.

Second overleaf: The figurines receive a second firing at 1040 degrees (celsius). When they emerge from the kiln they are very shiny. (Photo by Gerhard Skrobek)

Above: Minka Radiceu proudly holds a figurine she is carrying to the glazing bath.

Right: Brunhilde Schilling dips Umbrella Boy *into the glaze. Actually a neutral color, the glaze is given a slight green tint for quality control purposes so that on inspection, uncovered spots will show up white.*

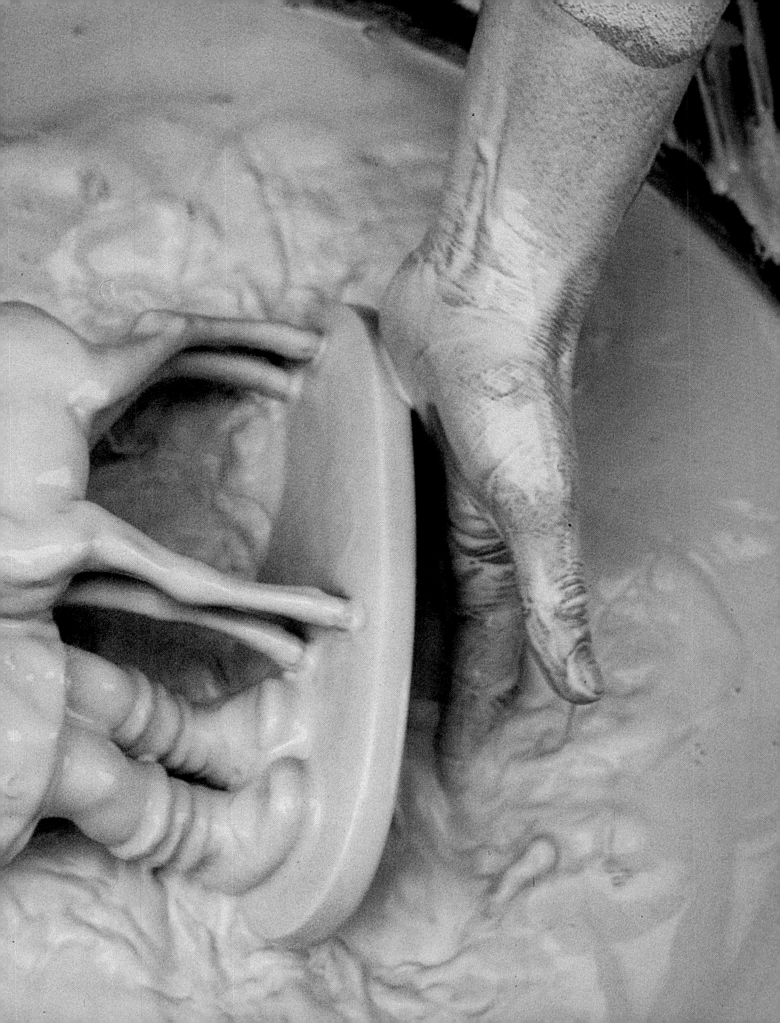

Top: Richard Wahner, ovenmaster, charges and empties the big electric kilns. Waldemar Jahn, above left, and Stefan Kühn, above right, are kiln department technicians. They make sure that their kilns are in top shape.

Left: Dieter Oursin heads the kiln department. He is the sixth generation of his family to work at Goebel.

Overleaf: Master Sample Painter Gunther Neubauer attempts to match ceramic paint samples with the colors on an Ars Edition M.I. Hummel card. Neubauer's selections will be painted on sample figurines, which will be taken to the Siessen Convent for review and possible approval. The convent reviews samples of the figurines so that form and colors hold to the likeness of Sister Maria Innocentia Hummel's published two-dimensional art.

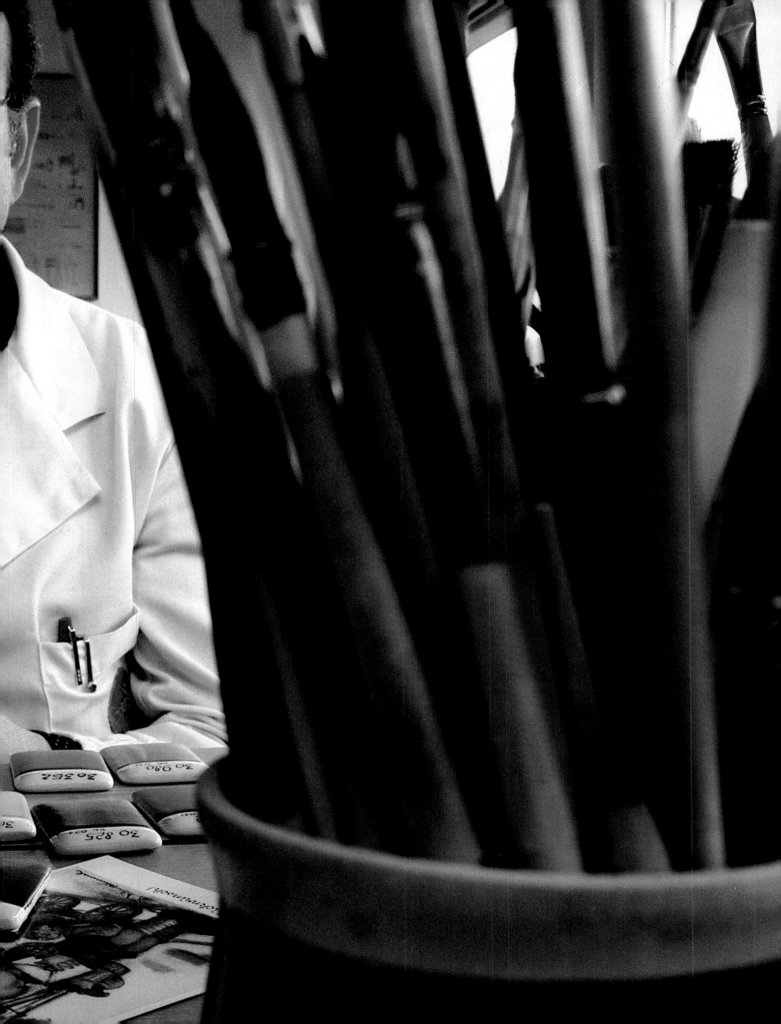

Above: Neubauer reviews the color samples in order to come as close as possible to the color of a card.

Left: A mosaic of ceramic color test samples at the paint lab.

Overleaf: The raw materials of paint making. The colors used on M.I. Hummel figurines require delicate preparation. Each formula is developed by Goebel's ceramic paint chemists.

Above and right: Painting department supervisor Gunther Bauer mixes some ceramic color powders with a quick drying oil to make a small amount of paint. These paints are made under strict quality controls, in small quantities,and are only given out to painters as needed.

*Left and above: A Merry Wanderer
face being painted. The colors
Neubauer chose and Bauer mixed
are now being applied by a painter.
It takes many years to earn the
position of face painter. Though
the face is shiny now a glaze firing
at low temperature will cause the
metallic oxide paint to melt into
the ceramic mass on firing, creating
a matte finish.*

*Overleaf: The signature of a master
painter being applied to a model
figurine.*

Top and above: Craftsmen paint
the bodies of M.I. Hummel
figurines. Each of these painters has
toured the United States as part of
Goebel's demonstration program.

Left: Edith Keilhammer paints a
doll's head.

Above: Steffen Schmidt, left, creates sample pieces for casting at Goebel. Bernd Schindhelm, right, is a member of the painting department. He has traveled often to the United States to demonstrate the art of painting M.I. Hummel figurines.

Right: Werner Rauch makes fine quality porcelain dinnerware at the Oeslauer Manufaktur, another part of the Goebel factory.

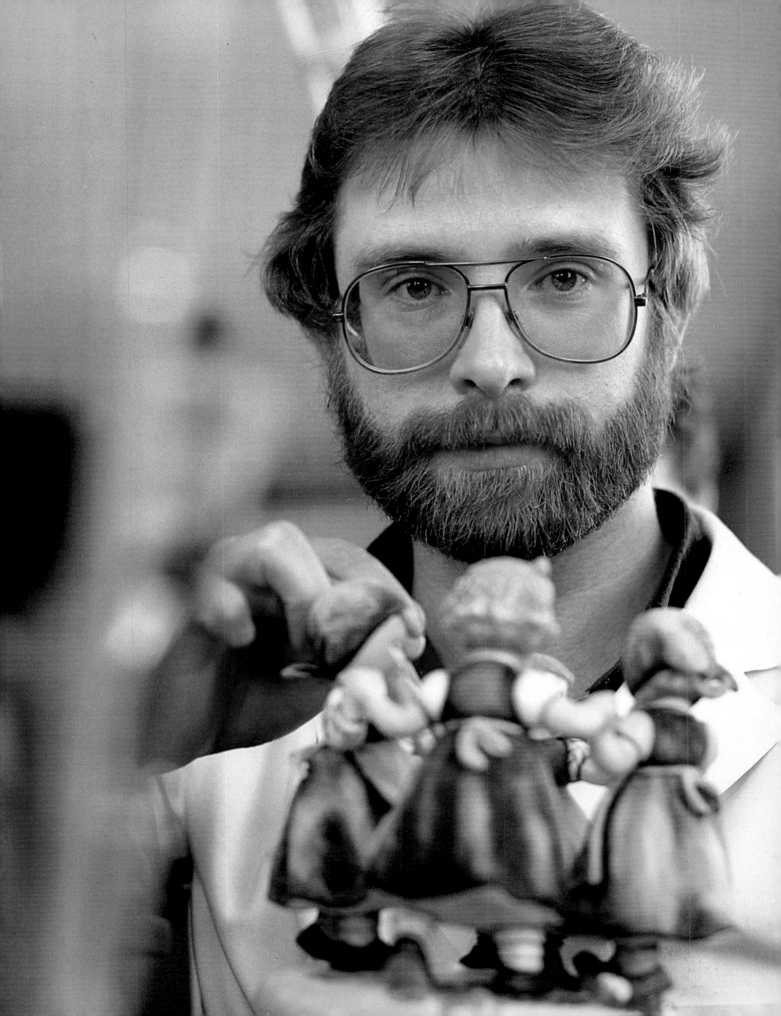

Above: Sigrid Borens is a painter of M.I. Hummel and other figurines at Goebel.

Left: Doris Schmieder paints M.I. Hummel figurines and wildlife birds.

Overleaf: Wolfgang Engel, a Goebel painter for over a quarter of a century, helps bring HUM 348, *Ring Around the Rosie, to life.*

Top and right: Still lifes from the factory.

Overleaf: HUM 258, *Which Hand? gets some finishing touches with a special skin tone paint developed by Goebel ceramic chemists. The paint helps give the figurines a soft character much like Sister Maria Innocentia's drawings and cards.*

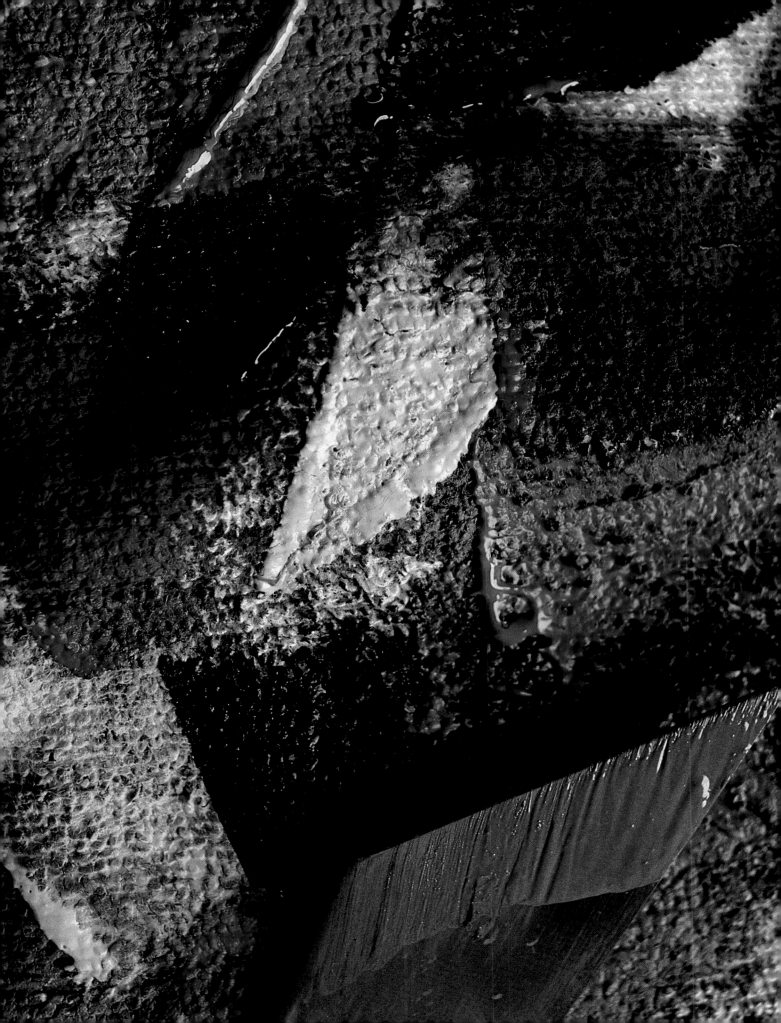

Overleaf: Master Sculptor Gerhard Skrobek works with the young students at the Goebel modeling school. Goebel recruits only the leading students from Germany's technical high school system and puts them through a difficult three-year apprenticeship program.

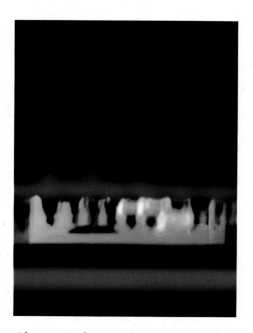

Above: Colors melt into the ceramic mass of a figurine during a glaze firing. The Master Sample Painter chooses the colors so that they will blend together during this firing, creating the matte colors that resemble closely Sister Maria Innocentia's published art cards and drawings, as well as some bright hues. Depending on the colors required, a figurine may be glaze fired as many as ten times.

Right: Gunther Meyer, chief of quality control, presides over more than 50 quality checkpoints.

Top: The students learn all phases of painting just as they would at art school. Then they are sent to the Bavarian State School for Porcelain in Selb for technical training. As they mature they will pass the Goebel tradition on to still another generation.

Above: Annette Renner celebrates her graduation from Goebel's apprenticeship program, her completed projects in front of her.

Left: Klaus Boehm, head of the Goebel painting school.

Overleaf: A portrait of Sister Maria Innocentia Hummel hangs in the Goebel painting school as a tribute to a proud tradition.

MALTECHNISCHE
BEGRIFFE

Num	Bezeichnung / Modelleur	Internat. Musterschutz	Deutscher Musterschutz	Kloster Sießen	
0345 X 1972	Der Kaufmann A Fair Measure (Skrobek) 5.6.72 Wehlte 14.8.56 14 cm Stehender Junge als Kaufmann hinter Bank, mit Waage ab- wiegend, auf rundem Post. Nr. Foto	18.7.57 4.12.72 ©	18.7.57 4.12.72	15.7.57 genehm.	
0346 1960 Nr. 5902	Das kluge Schwesterlein The smart little Sister Skrobek 22.10.56 11,5 cm Junge u. Mädchen auf Bank sitzend, Mädchen auf Schiefertafel schreibend auf Naturpostament	18.7.57 ©	18.7.57	15.7.57 genehmigt	
0347 1970 Nr. 14 239	Die sieben Schwaben Aventure Bound The seven Swabians Menzenbach 12.7.57 7 Jungen im Doppelreihe mit langem Spieß auf viereckigem Postament Größe 18,5 cm Post. 20,5 x 12 cm	8.10.57	8.10.57 ©	Ton Far... ge...	
0348 1957 Nr. 5619	Ringelreihen Ring a round the Rosie Skrobek 27.8.57 Höhe 18 cm, Post.-Ø 16,5 cm 4 Mädchen tanzend und sich an d. Händen haltend, rundes Post.	31.10.57	31.10.57 ©	farbig genehm.	
0349 1974 Nr. 4774	Der Blumenfreund The florist Skrobek 1.11.57 18 cm stehender Junge, an Blume in der Hand riechend, davor Busch m. Blumen u. Vogel ovales Postament	18.4.61 ©	18.4.61 (1960)	lt. Schreiben v. 20.2... u. Vogel weglass... genehmigt u... Ann m. Bl... 5...	

Postament

num	Bezeichnung / Modelleur	Int.echad. Mustersch.	Deutscher Mustersch.	Kloster Sießen	MM
)350 1980 ~1974~ r.5835	Zum Festtag On Holiday Skrobek 10.8.64 10,5 cm steh. Mädchen m. Korb u. Blumen a.l. Arm u. Regenschirm i.r. Hand. auf rundem Post.		9.9.65	Tonmodell am 23.10.64 genehmigt Farbiges Muster genehmigt am	MM ~20 w~ ~19 6~
)351 1982 ~1974~ r.5860	Enzianfreude The Botanist Skrobek 14.4.65 11 cm Sitz. Mädchen m. Enzian- kranz u. 1 Blüte i. d. Händen, Vogel z. Rechten auf Naturpostament	1972	~9.9.65~ 29.5.72	Tonmodell genehmigt 21.4.65 Farbiges Muster genehmigt am	MM ~72 w~ ~9 6~ 2
)352 1980 1974 r.5835	Ein süßer Gruß Sweet Greetings Skrobek 10.8.64 10,5 cm steh. Mädchen vor Zaun m. Lebkuchenherz auf ovalem Postament		9.9.65	Tonmodell am 23.10.64 genehmigt Farbiges Muster genehmigt am	MM ~20 w~ ~10 6~ 6
)353/0)15)353/I 17 cm 1963 nr Größe I 5619	~Sommertanz~ Frühlingstanz Skrobek 22.11.62 Spring Dance 2 Mädchen ohne Kopftuch von Hum 348 sich an den Händen fassend- tanzend ovales Post.	1963	1963 ©	genehmigt 20.5.63	MM KH
354 A 354 B 354 C	Weihbessel m. Engel " " " " " " " " wurden später als Fig. genehmigt 357, 358, 359 moth. v. Unger ausgeasb. v. Menzenbach	1961		} Konvkloster abgelehnt am 15.9.65	

One of the most interesting facets of any collecting hobby is the study of items that are classified as unique or rare, as opposed to regular production pieces. The intense fascination and excitement that variations and rarities create among dedicated M.I. Hummel collectors has done much to stimulate the tremendous growth of interest in worldwide M.I. Hummel figurine collecting.

Naturally, any discussion of rarities and uniqueness is a highly complex matter, and apt to be very controversial to a certain extent. This is very much the case where M.I. Hummel figurines are concerned. I know because—as a collector—I have been personally involved in buying and selling M.I. Hummel figurines for many years. In fact, most of the figurines shown in this chapter are from our personal collection.

While my appraisals and evaluations are obviously arbitrary and reflect my own interest as a collector, they are based upon years of experience. In general, they represent a consensus among my peers who are also deeply involved in the trading of M.I. Hummel figurines, as well as in the pure sense of collecting and connoisseurship that got most of us involved in the first place.

When it comes to placing a value on any rare or unusual specimen, a number of factors contribute to the general pricing scale. The age of the item in question is, understandably, one of the influencing factors (but not the foremost). A larger size does not always mean a higher value, because a smaller size could have been produced in lesser quantities, and thus be more valuable today. Perhaps the most significant factors in determining the value of any particular rarity would be the number of pieces known to have been produced under a certain style, and how the figurine in question seriously differs from the standard piece. A classic example is HUM 31, *Silent Night with Black Child*, which was produced in extremely limited quantities, discontinued and then re-introduced as HUM 54 without the black child. Only one known example in mint condition remains today, in our personal collection, making it perhaps the most rare and most valuable single M.I. Hummel figurine in the world.

While M.I. Hummel figurines have been produced since 1935, they were not popularly collected until the years following the Second World War and, until that time, the earlier wares of the Goebel factory competed with other decorative figurines for places in consumers' homes. Production records in early years were sketchy or non-existent, making it extremely difficult today to determine just how many specimens of any particular production run actually have survived the rigors of the years and remain in their original condition today.

Occasionally, an M.I. Hummel figurine that was once thought to be unique has to be downgraded to the rare category when another specimen is discovered (or several). This, however, does not *necessarily* reduce the value of the original. The ever-increasing numbers of M.I. Hummel collectors are always ready to wage a bidding war in an effort to obtain a rare figurine for their own collection!

It would be seriously remiss to leave the reader under the impression that all of the rare and unique M.I. Hummel figurines have already been discovered, for the exact opposite could well be true. The thousands of earlier-produced figurines have been scattered all over the world, with some, no doubt, in the hands of non-collectors who do not realize the significance and value of their possessions. It is here that the future discoveries of rare and unique M.I. Hummel figurines may lie. The story is still unfolding, day by day.

HUM 263 Merry Wanderer,
Wall Plaque (in relief)
This unique wall plaque, modeled by master sculptor Gerhard Skrobek in 1968, was made as a sample only and not produced for sale as an open edition. It is simply a Merry Wanderer (HUM 7/0) figurine made without a base, slightly flattened on the back side with a hole provided for hanging. The example in our collection has the incised number 263 and the "three line" trademark as well as the incised M.I. Hummel signature.

HUM 263 Merry Wanderer,
Wall Plaque (rear view)
To my knowledge, this is the first published photograph of the back view of this unusual prototype wall plaque. The front view photo does not give the appearance of depth that can be shown in this view. It looks like it would be possible for a collector to make such a plaque by taking HUM 7/0, Merry Wanderer, removing the base and grinding the back so that it would hang flat against the wall. But then, of course, you would not have the incised number or signature, nor the "three line" trademark!

HUM 1 Puppy Love
This figurine has the distinction of being Number 1 in the M.I. Hummel numbering system, and is very similar in design to HUM 2 and HUM 4, except for the reddish-brown terrier. The figurine on the left may be an early prototype and it is doubtful that it was produced in any great quantity with the boy's head in this position. It does not compare accurately with Sister Maria Innocentia Hummel's sketch, which would be more like the current version, shown on the right. The prototype has no tie while her sketch definitely depicts a blue tie on the fiddler.

HUM 107 Little Fiddler Plaque
HUM 106 Merry Wanderer
Plaque (with wood frame)
These two extremely rare wall plaques were modeled in 1938 by master sculptor Arthur Möller. Both were produced in very limited quantities and have an incised "crown" trademark as well as the incised number 106 or 107. This matched pair was purchased in Germany shortly after World War II by a U.S. Army officer from Columbus, Ohio. There is a variation in the wood frames of some models, but this does not affect the value if they are in otherwise good condition.

HUM 187 W.G.P. "Service" Plaque
(Special)
This service plaque was first introduced in the late 1950's and has become a Goebel tradition. Each employee of W. Goebel Porzellanfabrik, regardless of his or her position or department, receives this special plaque on the occasion of his or her 25th, 40th and 50th anniversary with Goebel.

HUM 208, 209, 213 M.I. Hummel Dealer's Plaques
M.I. Hummel figurines have been sold in many countries. In the early 1950's most stores were provided with a small ceramic sign stating that they were selling the original M.I. Hummel product made by Goebel. These little "dealer's plaques" were made in several different languages. Those in French, Swedish and Spanish are shown here. Depending on wording and condition, they normally sell in the $2,000 to $3,000 price range. Since the mid-1960's only dealer's plaques in English have been used.

264

HUM 211 M.I. Hummel Dealer's Plaque

This is probably the rarest of all M.I. Hummel dealer's plaques. The only known painted example was located in 1975 by Major Larry Spohn and his wife Anne while they were living in Germany and is now in the Robert L. Miller collection. All the lettering on this plaque is in lower case and the word "Oeslau" is used as the location of W. Goebel Porzellanfabrik. It was modeled in 1950 by master sculptor Reinhold Unger. The exact purpose or reason for designing this plaque still remains a mystery today.

HUM 211 M.I. Hummel Dealer's Plaque (unpainted)

Shown here is an unpainted model of the HUM 211 *dealer's plaque. Several of these unfinished plaques were located in the Goebel factory and at least two examples are known to be in the hands of private collectors. Notice the quotation marks around the word "Hummel" on this rare version.*

HUM 210 M.I. Hummel Dealer's Plaque

This is a normal dealer's plaque in English with "Schmid Bros. Inc. Boston" embossed on the side of the satchel of the Merry Wanderer. This extremely rare plaque was first modeled in 1950 by master sculptor Reinhold Unger. It was made with a dotted "i" and without quotation marks. Very few are known to exist. Schmid Bros. was one of the early importers of M.I. Hummel figurines. This plaque is valued at over $5,000.

HUM 180 Tuneful Good Night,
Wall Plaque
*Happy Bugler was the original
name given to this colorful wall
plaque. It was apparently
produced in small quantities in
the early trademark periods as
attested by the scarcity of "crown"
and "full bee" examples on the
secondary market. It was again
produced in quantity in the late
1970's and is now in the current
production program. The plaque
was recently restyled in 1981 and
the slightly changed version
appears on the right in this
photograph.*

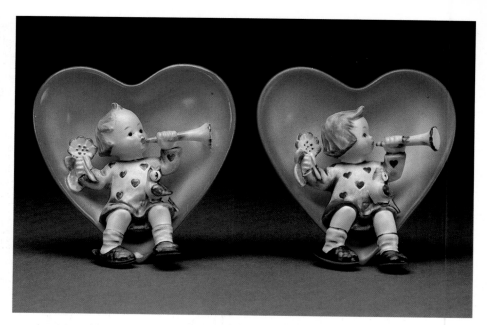

HUM 137 Child in Bed,
Wall Plaque
HUM 138 Tiny Baby in Crib,
Wall Plaque
HUM 139 Flitting Butterfly,
Wall Plaque
*The Tiny Baby in Crib wall plaque,
center, is extremely rare. According
to old factory records, this small
plaque was never produced for
sale. The other two models are still
in current production in slightly
different forms. Early models of
HUM 137 had an incised letter "B"
after the number, indicating that it
was intended to be a set. To this
date, an example of HUM 137 A has
never been located.*

"Mel" Signature Items
*Not all sample model M.I.
Hummel design figurines are
approved for final production.
Such is the case with the items
pictured here. In order that the
initial design costs were not totally
lost, the items were later marked
with the "Mel" name incised—
which is actually the last three
letters of Hummel.*

The Flying Bumblebee

In 1950, four years after the death of Sister Maria Innocentia Hummel, the Goebel factory wished to pay tribute to her fine artistry in some way. They radically changed the trademark, instituting the use of a bee flying high with a "V." (Hummel means "bumblebee" in German, and the "V" stands for "Verkaufsgesellschaft" or distribution company.) This trademark, known as the "full bee," was used in various forms for many years. The two ceramic items shown here were used as selling tools to promote M.I. Hummel products.

Walt Disney Items

Little known is the fact that the Goebel factory made many other lines of figurines besides the M.I. Hummel figurines. A series of Walt Disney items were produced in the early 1950's, totaling over 140 different items. These old pieces with the "full bee" trademark are now collector's items. Some Walt Disney designs are still in current production.

Norman Rockwell Items

Another line of figurines produced in the early 1960's was a series of eighteen different figurines from the original drawings of Norman Rockwell. Possibly they were much ahead of their time, as figurine collecting had not reached today's height of popularity. The line of figurines was discontinued after a few years. To my knowledge, only twelve models were actually produced for sale, and possibly as few as 500 of each were made—truly a limited edition by today's standards.

HUM 181, 189, 190, 191 The Mamas and the Papas

These M.I. Hummel figurines, bearing the "authentic" signature, were made in 1948 by master sculptor Arthur Möller, but never went into production. They were not considered typical of Sister Maria Innocentia's work, although they are exact replicas of some of her early sketches. This is the only set known to be in a private collection; a similar set is in the Goebel factory archives. The set is often referred to as the "Mamas and the Papas," so named by my wife, Ruth. They are now in the Robert L. Miller collection.

HUM 181 Old Man Reading Newspaper
HUM 202 Old Man Reading Newspaper, Table Lamp

Master sculptor Arthur Möller was apparently fascinated with this design and decided it should also be made as a table lamp. Approval for production was not authorized. The only other known example of this piece is on display in the Goebel factory archives in Rödental, West Germany.

HUM 87 For Father

Originally called Father's Joy *when it was first modeled by master sculptor Arthur Möller in 1938, this piece can usually be located in all six trademarks with only minor variations. The boy is carrying white radishes and a beer stein. The only major variation is that some models have orange-colored vegetables that would appear to be carrots, as shown on the right. The orange carrot variation normally sells in the $500 to $1,000 price range and is difficult to locate on the secondary market.*

HUM 831, 832 International Designs

The figurines shown on this page and on the following one were designed in 1940. They are all prototypes that were made in native costumes of various countries for possible sale in each of those countries. Due to the events of World War II, production of the International Figurines series was not started. Only a few examples are known to exist today. This photograph shows the figurines in Slovak-style costumes, designed by master sculptor Reinhold Unger.

HUM 824, 825 International Designs

These figurines in Swedish-style costumes were designed by master sculptor Arthur Möller.

HUM 842, 841 International Designs

These figurines in Czech-style costumes were designed by master sculptor Reinhold Unger.

HUM 809, 810, 807 International Designs

These figurines in Bulgarian-style costumes were designed by master sculptor Arthur Möller.

HUM 852, 851, 854, 853
International Designs

These figurines in Hungarian-style costumes were designed by master sculptor Arthur Möller.

HUM 968, 968, 947, 904, 913, 812 **International Designs**

These figurines in Serbian-style costumes were all designed by master sculptor Reinhold Unger, except for HUM 947, which was designed by Arthur Möller.

HUM 74 Little Gardener

Little Gardener *was originally modeled by master sculptor Reinhold Unger in 1937 and has undergone many changes over the years, both in color and design. The older models have an oval base, while the newer model has a round base and a smaller flower, as shown on the right. These changes are interesting, but are not considered unusually rare, as they can be readily located on the secondary market.*

HUM 17 Congratulations

Congratulations *has been produced in all trademark periods since 1935. It was originally made in two sizes. The large size was apparently made in very limited quantities and is extremely difficult to find today; it often sells for over $5,000 when found with the "crown" trademark. The small size was restyled in 1971 by master sculptor Gerhard Skrobek, who added socks, a new hair style and a more textured finish to the dress. The new style is shown on the right.*

HUM 311 Kiss Me

Often it is only a small change in design that makes one figurine more valuable than another. Such is the case with Kiss Me. *Shown on the left is the original version as it was first introduced in the U.S. market in 1961. In 1963 it was redesigned to make the doll slightly smaller in size so that it would look more like a doll and less like a child. This little change makes a difference of $300 to $500 between the old and the new models among collectors.*

HUM 154 Waiter

This popular figurine was first produced in 1943 as it appears on the right, with gray coat and gray-striped trousers. In the early 1950's the colors were changed to a blue coat and tan-striped trousers, and it was produced with various names on the bottle. "Rhein-wine" or "Rhein Wine" are the most common. "Whisky," "Hiher Mchie" and other illegible names have been used. These various names make Waiter a very popular collectible.

HUM 53 Joyful

The old "crown" trademark version shown on the left is extremely rare because of the color variation. Note the orange dress and blue shoes. This popular figurine has been produced in one basic size only but has varied greatly in size through the years as shown by the two center examples. The current production model is shown on the extreme right and now has a brownish-colored mandolin.

HUM 345, 308, 327, 314, 337

Not all rare and unusual M.I. Hummel figurines are old. The five figurines shown here were all put on the market in 1972. Shortly after their release, each item was restyled in design, with various minor changes. Most serious collectors want to have an example of both the old and new models in their collection.

272

HUM 13 Meditation

This figurine is a collector's delight. It was originally made in two sizes only: HUM 13/0 and HUM 13/2. It has been restyled several times and has numerous size variations as well as variations in the girl's hair ribbons and pigtails. The rarest and most difficult size to locate would be the figurine with the flowers in the back half of the basket. This model, when found in near mint condition, often brings over $3,000 on the secondary market.

HUM 340 Letter to Santa Claus

The evolution of a M.I. Hummel design is shown here. Letter to Santa Claus was originally designed by master sculptor Helmut Wehlte in 1956 as it is shown on the left. The center figurine shows a major restyling as it appeared a year or two later. Finally, a third restyling by master sculptor Gerhard Skrobek in 1970 produced the model on the right. This is the model that was actually put on the market in 1972. There are only two known prototype models in existence today—the other one is owned by collectors in California.

HUM 214/E, 220 We Congratulate

This photograph shows two different figurines with different numbers but the same name: We Congratulate. The figurine shown on the right, HUM 220, has the normal base that most of the figurines have. Shown on the left is the same figurine, HUM 214/E, without the base as it is produced for display as part of the nativity set. The rear view shows the normal incised M.I. Hummel signature on the figurine at the left, while the center figurine has a painted signature rather than an incised one. This example is considered unusual rather than rare.

HUM 65 Farewell

Farewell *was originally modeled in 1937 by master sculptor Arthur Möller in one size only, as shown on the left. In the mid-1950's plans were made to produce it in two sizes—HUM 65/I and 65/0 —but apparently only a few sample pieces of the small 65/0 were actually produced. For that reason, this small size shown on the right is extremely rare and difficult to locate. Farewell is currently produced in only one size with the incised number 65 only.*

HUM 153 Auf Wiedersehn

Auf Wiedersehn *was originally modeled by master sculptor Arthur Möller in 1943 and was produced in the large size only. The small size was introduced in the early 1950's with the boy wearing a green hat and waving his hand. It is always found with the "full bee" trademark and "0" size designator directly under the number "153" and is considered rare because of the small amount produced in this style. It was later restyled and is still being produced as it appears on the right. A good specimen of the "boy wearing a hat" model is valued at $2,500 today.*

HUM 72 Spring Cheer

Shown in the center is the original model of Spring Cheer, an exact copy of Sister Maria Innocentia's original drawing. In 1965 it was restyled by master sculptor Gerhard Skrobek, who added flowers to her right hand and changed the color of her dress to dark green as it appears on the right. A few of the old-style models were subsequently found and given the darker colors, as shown on the left. These are quite rare and will usually command a premium when found.

HUM 174 She Loves Me, She Loves Me Not!

This ever-popular motif has undergone numerous changes over the years, since it was first modeled by master sculptor Arthur Möller in 1945. This photograph points out the change in the feather on the boy's hat, as well as the fact that the boy's eyes are now looking down at the flower rather than straight ahead, as they were in the older model shown on the left.

HUM 219 Little Velma
HUM 105 Adoration with Bird

The figurine on the left, unofficially known as Little Velma, was produced in very limited quantities, possibly less than 50 pieces. It is believed that the total production was shipped to, and sold only in, Canada. It is named in honor of the lady who first brought it to the attention of, and sold it to, me. Two variations of HUM 105 are shown. Notice the position of the braid on the girl. Both examples are rare, very limited production and discontinued items that were never shown in old M.I. Hummel catalogues.

HUM 99 Eventide
HUM 28 Wayside Devotion

Old factory records indicate that Eventide was first produced in 1938. It is almost identical to HUM 28, Wayside Devotion, shown on the right, the major difference being the shrine. On the left is a rare variation of Eventide (with "crown" trademark) with the lambs centered in front of the two children. All standard Eventides would have the lambs slightly to the right when the viewer is facing the figurine. The rare version would command a premium on the secondary market.

HUM 104 Eventide, Table Lamp
HUM 100 Shrine, Table Lamp
*This extremely rare lamp base
shown on the right is similar to the
figurine* HUM 23, Adoration. *It was
modeled by Erich Lautensack in
1938 and produced in very limited
quantities. Pictured on the left is
the only known example of* HUM
104, Eventide *Table Lamp that was
purchased from its original owner
in northern Indiana and is now
part of the Robert L. Miller
Collection. Notice the position of
the lambs directly in front of the
children.*

HUM 101 To Market, Table Lamp
*On the extreme left is an early
prototype model of the To Market
lamp base with the rare plain post.
It was redesigned in the early
1950's with the "tree trunk" post as
shown in the center, with the
incised number 101. Master
sculptor Arthur Möller redesigned
this lamp again in 1952 into the
9½-inch size with the incised
number 223. This design, shown
on the right, is still being produced.*

HUM 231, 234 Birthday Serenade,
Table Lamp
*The two pieces on the left are still
in current production and are
readily available. The two on the
right are rare. The major difference
is the reversal of the musical
instruments between the new and
old models.* HUM 234 *is the incised
number of the 7¾-inch size, while*
HUM 231 *is the incised number on
the 9¾-inch model. The lamp base
shown on the right is the most
difficult to locate.*

HUM 103 Farewell, Table Lamp
HUM 102 Volunteers, Table Lamp
The two extremely rare lamp bases shown here were both modeled in 1937 and were produced in very limited quantities. The specimen of HUM 102, Volunteers, on the right was found in 1979 in Seattle, Washington, in a thrift shop and purchased by an alert collector for less than $20 in that city. HUM 103, Farewell lamp base shown on the left, is equally rare, with only five or six examples currently known to exist in collector's hands.

HUM 325, 326, 338 (PFE)
The three possible future edition (PFE) figurines in this group photograph were produced as samples only almost thirty years ago. So far, they have not been produced in quantity for sale as an open edition for M.I. Hummel enthusiasts to purchase. It is doubtful if they ever will, but then, who knows? Anything is possible when it comes to M.I. Hummel collecting. These three examples were sent to New York for copyright purposes, were lost for many years, and then turned up on the secondary market, for sale to the highest bidder.

HUM 9 Begging His Share
This figurine was originally produced in 1935 as a candleholder with a hole in the center of the cake in which to insert a wax candle. The figurine was reduced slightly in size when it was restyled in 1964 and has been produced ever since with a solid cake without the hole for the candle. Note the brightly colored socks on the early "crown" trademarked piece pictured in the center. This figurine is still in current production and now appears like the one shown on the left.

HUM 192 Candlelight,
Candleholder

Carrier of Light, as it was named in older catalogues, was originally modeled by master sculptor Reinhold Unger in 1948 with a long red ceramic candle reaching to the angel's feet. It was later restyled in 1958 with a short candleholder ending in the angel's hands. The older models are slightly larger and can usually be found for sale in the $500 to $750 price range.

HUM 37 Herald Angels,
Candleholder

This candleholder was originally modeled in 1935 by master sculptor Reinhold Unger and is still in the current production program today. There have been many variations over the years—note the taller candleholder and smaller base on the older model on the left. The order of placement of the angels may vary on the older models, but they are always in the same position on the current production model.

HUM 113 Heavenly Song,
Candleholder
HUM 31 Silent Night with
Black Child, Candleholder
HUM 54 Silent Night,
Candleholder

HUM 31 is probably the rarest and most talked-about M.I. Hummel figurine today. Apparently only a few samples were produced in 1935; this is one of the few known existing mint condition specimens. It was part of the collection of Mrs. Viktoria Hummel, the late mother of Sister Maria Innocentia. HUM 113, left, is a closed edition (discontinued); HUM 54 is the version currently being produced.

278

HUM 27 Joyous News
HUM 32 Little Gabriel

Little Gabriel *is shown along with the seated version. In fact,* Little Gabriel *was called* Joyous News *in some old catalogues.* Little Gabriel *was originally produced in two sizes, 32/0 and 32/I. The large size,* HUM 32/I, *was discontinued and is now considered extremely rare. The small size was restyled in 1982. The small 27/I,* Joyous News *candleholder (extreme left), was discontinued in the early 1950's and is now considered extremely rare in good condition. It was later reduced slightly in size and given the number 40/I.*

HUM 301 Christmas Angel (PFE)

A possible future edition (PFE) is a figurine that has been designed and approved for production and possible release at a future date. The beautiful Christmas Angel, *originally called* Delivery Angel, *is such a figurine. It was modeled in 1957 and has an early "stylized" trademark. This example was purchased a number of years ago in Germany.*

HUM 42 Good Shepherd

This delightful motif was modeled in 1935 by master sculptor Reinhold Unger and was originally produced in two sizes. The large size, 42/I, was produced in very limited quantities and then discontinued completely in the early 1950's. It is considered extremely rare and a good "crown" trademarked specimen will normally sell for appoximately $5,000. The figurine shown on the right is an excellent Japanese copy. Even the experienced collector is sometimes fooled by such unauthorized copies.

HUM 172 Festival Harmony
(Mandolin)

This photograph shows the various changes that have taken place in the production of this beautiful angel figurine. The old "crown" trademarked piece on the left is the earliest style produced. It was restyled in the early 1950's with the bird resting on the mandolin and flowers on the hem of the angel's gown, and then restyled again in the late 1960's with the new textured finish and flowers placed at the angel's feet. The small size (172/0) was modeled in 1961 and is found in one style only.

HUM 173 Fesitval Harmony
(Flute)

This is a companion piece to the angle with mandolin (HUM 172) and was first modeled in 1947 by master sculptor Reinhold Unger. The old crown trademarked piece on the left is the earliest style produced. It was restyled in the early 1950's, and then restyled again in the late 1960's. The two current production figurines are on the right. There have been some minor color variations through the years, but these only tend to enhance the beauty of this figurine.

Unnumbered M.I. Hummel Figurine

This unusual, extremely rare, signed M.I. Hummel figurine is a collector's dream come true. Found several years ago in Munich, Germany, this beautiful Madonna with Wings figurine had been in the possession of a German family for many years, but they could not remember its background or where it came from. The figurine is not numbered nor does it have a trademark, only an incised "X" on the bottom, in addition to the M.I. Hummel signature on the back that makes this figurine unique, rare and fascinating.

HUM 214/A Madonna and Child

In 1951 when the M.I. Hummel nativity set was first modeled by Reinhold Unger, the figurine of the Virgin Mary and Infant Jesus was designed in one piece, with the incised number 214 A. Because of production problems it was later produced as two separate pieces, both with the same number (214 A) incised on the bottom of each piece. This is the only known instance where two different pieces have the same incised number. The one-piece unit was sold in white overglaze finish as well as the full color finish. Both are considered rare today.

HUM 10 Flower Madonna

This beautiful Flower Madonna figurine is the most popular madonna figurine ever produced in ceramic form. It has been in constant production since it was first put on the market in 1935 and has appeared in many sizes as well as color variations. Originally it was modeled by master sculptor Reinhold Unger with an open halo, which was later changed to a closed halo when it was restyled in 1956. The pastel yellow, brown cloak and ivory finish are quite rare and extremely difficult to find. The white overglaze and pastel blue are the colors produced today.

HUM 55 Saint George

This is not a typical M.I. Hummel figurine, but it is based upon a sketch by Sister Maria Innocentia. The drawing of St. George upon which it is based was recently found in a 1935 German edition of a book about M.I. Hummel. The old "crown" trademark version with the bright red saddle on the left is rare and very difficult to locate. St. George has been produced in one size only and has changed only slightly through the years other than the color of the saddle. It is still in current production as shown on the right.

SISTER MARIA INNOCENTIA HUMMEL REMEMBERED

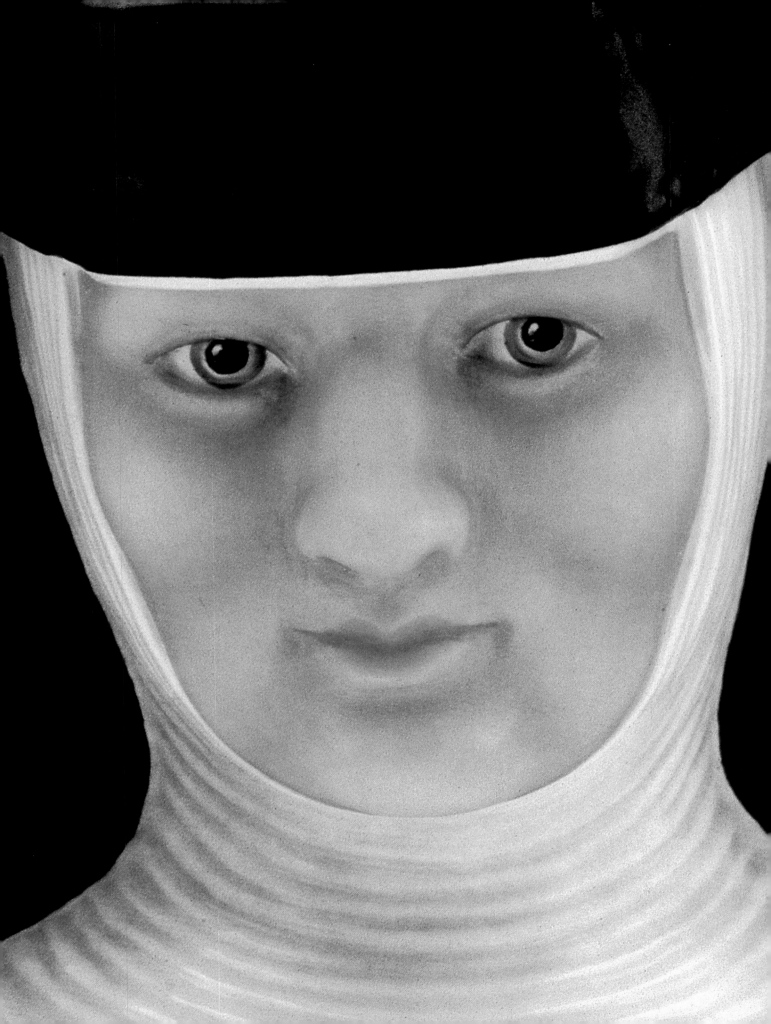

Preceding page: A detail of HU 3, a
bust of Sister Maria Innocentia
Hummel, created for members of
the Goebel Collectors' Club in
1979.

Opposite page: A self-portrait by
the artist, done before she entered
Siessen.

A Universal Appeal

Sister Maria Innocentia Hummel is one of a handful of 20th-century
artists whose work enjoys popularity with a very broad spectrum of
American society. Like Norman Rockwell, Grandma Moses and
Andrew Wyeth, she devoted a great part of her life to the development
of a unique artistic style that captured the world in which she lived.
But her images were not those of Main Street, U.S.A., or the stark
Pennsylvania Dutch country landscapes that characterized Rockwell
and Wyeth; they were a continent and a culture away. Sister Maria
Innocentia was German, and deeply attached to the folklore of both
rural Lower Bavaria, where she spent her childhood, and of the
Swabian Alps around the Siessen Convent, where she lived and drew
during her adult life. How was it then the the work of this artist, who
spent an important part of her life in a Franciscan convent, has come to
achieve such widespread popularity in the United States? What are
the key elements in the substance of her work that appeal to so many
people from different walks of life?

"The main focus of Sister Maria Innocentia's non-religious art is clearly
on the image and spirit of the child," says Professor Dr. Ulrich Gertz, a
noted German art historian and specialist in porcelain, ceramics and
sculpture. "It develops out of three sources running through her
life. First, the feeling of universal love that was stressed in her religious
life. Second, the images and memories of the freedom of her own
childhood in rural Lower Bavaria. Third, her frequent contact with
children as an art teacher at Siessen and with the children from nearby
towns who visited her at the convent on Sunday afternoons so that
they might be sketched. We can look at the faces of Sister Maria
Innocentia's children, accordingly, as a mixture of reality and ideal.
They have a particular animation that makes them come alive in the
mind of the most casual observer and create sparks of emotion."

Had Sister Maria Innocentia not suffered a tragic death in 1946, she
might have offered the answers to some of these questions herself.
We do know, however, that she held a particular curiosity about the
United States, and in a letter dated October 18, 1939, she wrote Ars
Sacra, her card publisher in Munich, concerning a series of Christmas
cards she was to draw, and asked, "in what fashion should I draw
for America?" The publisher's response was simple and to the point. "For
America you need not work any differently than for Germany...."

This reassurance, at a time when her work had gained a modest
following in the United States in the forms of figurines and art cards,
suggests that the universal appeal of her images had started to develop
during her own lifetime. And it is the strength of this universality that
is the main contributor to the success of Sister Maria Innocentia's
art, establishing her work clearly as a genre of its own. And though
there have been numerous attempts to imitate her style and themes,
all are lacking in the spirit and devotion that were the true hallmarks of
the artist.

A Bavarian Childhood

The artist was born Berta Hummel, the third child of merchant Adolf
Hummel and his wife, Viktoria, on May 21, 1909, in the Bavarian
village of Massing an der Rott. Massing, like many rural Bavarian towns,
served as a market center, and the Hummels' general store was the
local commercial hub. On market days, farmers dressed in traditional
Bavarian folk costumes would come to sell their goods, swap stories

and tell jokes. These colorful, early childhood images of market day in Bavaria made a strong impression on the young girl.

Berta Hummel was a *Schauerfreitag*, gifted, as old Bavarian legend has it, with a vivid imagination. And true to this ancient legend, Berta instinctively picked up pencil and paper and started sketching as a young child. Observing this creative energy, Viktoria Hummel gave her daughter the nickname "das Hummele," the German for little bumblebee, because Berta was often buzzing from one creative impulse to another. And her father, who as a young man was forced to submerge his own ambition to become an artist in order to run the family business, established an extremely permissive homelife atmosphere with the hope that someday Berta might become the artist that he did not have the time to be.

But this permissive home environment did little to help Berta's progress at the Massing *Volksschule* (similar to the American country schoolhouse), where children between the ages of six and fifteen sat in the same classroom, and discipline was the order of the day. And it was only under the watchful eye of Sister Theresa, a member of the Order of Notre Dame, that young Berta developed a sense of self-discipline to complement her artistic talent. Sister Theresa encouraged Berta in her art, and wrote a strong letter of recommendation that helped her gain admission to the *Institut der Englischen Fraulein* (Institute of English Sisters), a well-respected boarding school in the town of Simbach, some twenty miles east of Massing.

Simbach boasted a full-scale art department with a cadre of teachers who helped to refine Berta's instinctive skills. She developed an interest in watercolor. She worked hard to develop her sketching technique by doing pen and pencil illustrations of fairy tale characters. And when school recessed for the summer she would often spend time vacationing at the home of an aunt in the resort town of Berchtesgaden in the Bavarian Alps.

"Berta would sketch and paint the mountain scenery for hours," her mother, Viktoria, who died in 1983, remembered. "Both her father and I began to sense a change. She was doing much more than sketches of her classmates and the little fantasies that used to take place around the house. The progress made her father very proud."

Just as Sister Theresa at the Massing *Volksschule* had recognized Berta's potential, so Sister Stephania at Simbach quickly saw her talent, and devoted a great deal of time to giving her the encouragement and confidence she needed to become an artist. Sister Stefania became Berta's mentor at Simbach. And through this student-mentor relationship, Berta received religious inspiration as well. "Berta began coming home with religious anecdotes and biblical tales instead of the fairy tales that had amused her so much when she was home," her mother remembered.

By 1925, when she was in her final year at Simbach, sixteen-year-old Berta had progressed sufficiently with her own art studies to be given the opportunity to assist Sister Stephania in the instruction of students in the lower grades.

Then graduation neared, and Berta had to look to the future. Germany in the 1920's was a nation of political, economic and cultural uncertainty, and the life of an aspiring young artist could not be expected to be an easy one. Sister Stephania counseled Adolf and Viktoria Hummel to send Berta to the *Akademie der Angewandte Kunst* (Academy of Applied Arts) in Munich. Berta was accepted at the

Sister Maria Innocentia's classical training and her frequent visits to Munich's Alte Pinakothek *to study the Old Masters are evident in her* Mother of God.

Academy for the term commencing in the fall of 1927. She was barely eighteen when she took the train to the Bavarian capital—an impressionable, sensitive young woman, whose talent as an artist was leading her on a new adventure in life.

Munich: New Styles and Influences

Berta's program at the Academy of Applied Arts in Munich was among the best being offered in Europe at the time. The director of the Academy was Professor Carlo Sattler, an architect and ceramic artist. Along with several of the professors there, Sattler was a member of *Der Deutsche Werkbund*—a professional association of teachers, artists, designers and architects who exerted a strong influence on the applied arts in general, and on their institutions of learning in particular. Berta's curriculum reflected the influence of *Werkbund*, as well as some of the ideas and innovations of the *Wiener Werkstatte*, a similar group with roots in Vienna whose influence spread to other cultural centers.

"The artist's curriculum at the Munich Academy brought her in direct contact with the people and ideas that were influencing the art scene at the time," says art historian Professor Dr. Gertz. "This contact, combined with frequent visits to Munich's famous *Alte Pinakothek*, helped Berta Hummel move toward the development of her own true style."

Just about a five-minute walk from the Academy, the *Alte Pinakothek* was the most famous art museum in Bavaria. There, Berta, along with her fellow students in the color and composition class of Professor Richard Klein, studied the works of Albrecht Dürer, Rubens, Van Dyck, EL Greco and Murillo. These visits to the museum brought her close to the old masters for the first time. This exposure also served to broaden her scope of artistic vision beyond the borders of Germany. "She talked of wanting to go to Florence or Venice to study and paint," her mother remembered.

Berta attended the *Berufsfachschule*, a special section of the Academy that offered a curriculum to prospective teachers of general art in elementary and high schools. Here, she had the opportunity to work in a secular environment for the first time. She studied drawing with Professor Max Dasio, well known for his illustrations in children's books and his woodcuts of German folklore characters.

"Dasio was definitely her most important influence at the Academy," Otto Hufnagel, a former classmate remembered. "He and Berta were both quick-witted, and it was this match of wits that saw them get along so well." As to Berta's relationship with the other students, Hufnagel recalled: "There are people who arrive at a new school and talk about their past exploits; but Berta Hummel wasn't that way. She made a quick impression on fellow students and professors with her excellent sketching technique. She was quiet, very pretty, and in my opinion a bit withdrawn from the social life that went along with school. Of course, this might have been due to her small-town background and the years she spent away from home in strict religious schools; but at the same time she was clever, possessing a fantastic humor and quick wit that would pop up when you least expected it."

Berta progressed through the *Berufsfachschule* curriculum, which included the watercolor class of Professor Else Brauneis; drawing with Professor Max Dasio; color and composition with Professor Richard Klein; nature drawing with Professor Friedrich Wirnhier; and art history with Dr. Hans Kiener. Her routine in Munich was broken from time to time thanks to the field trips that were part of Professor Brauneis' watercolor class. Berta journeyed to Salzburg, the old Austrian town famous for Mozart and its wonderful countryside, and to the towns of Garmisch and Partenkirchen in the Bavarian Alps. But these were only occasional ventures into the secular world, for the atmosphere at the religious dormitory run by the order of the Holy Family in Munich's Blumenstrasse was very strict and, once home, Berta would often turn her thoughts toward religious reflection.

Living in the Holy Family dormitory, Berta developed friendships with two sisters from a Franciscan convent at Siessen, near the town of Saulgau in the Swabian Alps. Sister Laura and Sister Cantalicia were also taking courses at the Munich Academy of Applied Arts. Through them, Berta learned about Siessen, where art was one of many subjects being taught to sisters who received training for duty as teachers in Franciscan-operated schools around Germany and overseas. And as she looked to the secular world for role models, Berta found, more and more, that her interests were shifting instead toward religious life.

"Berta had sent us letters telling us about her friendship with the two Franciscan sisters," her mother remembered. "When she invited them home to visit it became apparent to us that she might be considering the idea of joining the convent."

After eight semesters at the Munich Academy for Applied Arts, Berta made the decision to enter the Franciscan convent at Siessen. Many of her classmates and professors were surprised by her decision.

"Berta's decision to enter the convent was one that pleased my husband and me very much," Viktoria Hummel recalled. "We knew how much she wanted to live the life of an artist, but allowing herself to combine her religion with her art seemed more important. Her relationship with Sister Laura and Sister Cantalicia was an important factor in her decision to enter the convent. And Sister Theresa at the Massing *Volksschule* and Sister Stephania at Simbach gave her a great deal of strength and encouragement to continue with her art."

Berta's schooling at the Academy during the period 1927 through 1931 helped refine her natural skills as an artist to the point where she could apply her talents to almost any challenge in the art world. Her main areas of study—painting, drawing and composition—were her strongest, and in each she received the grade "1," the highest mark attainable. Her exposure to the *Werkbund* movement, which was attempting to create a fusion between the tradition of religious art and contemporary design in the predominantly Catholic urban cultural areas of central Europe, enriched her artistic perspective. And through her field trips she was able to keep in contact with the rural ambiance she had grown to know and love as a child.

First Years at Siessen
Berta Hummel entered the Siessen Convent on April 22, 1931. Her first duties were helping to design religious vestments and banners. At the teachers' school, she taught art to young children during this early period as a Franciscan postulant.

Also during this period the artist was invited to display her work at various seminars and gatherings of lay and religious primary school teachers. Her work had been found to be helpful in establishing the rapport between teacher and young student that is so essential in the development of the building blocks of primary education. After one such symposium, the small religious publishing house *ver Sacrum*

Sister Maria Innocentia's drawing,
Altar Picture, *was done during the
1930's.*

in the town of Rottenberg am Neckar expressed an interest in her work and, while she was still a postulant, became her publisher. Later, her work was also published by a handful of other religious art publishers including: The Society for Christian Art; Alfons Faulhaber Publishers; Gustav Mandt Publishers; and Ars Sacra/Verlag Josef Muller.

This work included religious illustrations, as well as other motifs featuring children and offering religious sayings and reminders, as well as secular motifs. Thus the art of the young Franciscan, published in various forms, began gaining a following around Germany, particularly in Bavaria and Swabia, both areas with large Catholic populations.

"Clearly, the artist's frequent contact with young children in their formative years was a strong incentive for her to exercise her outstanding sketching technique," says Professor Dr. Gertz. "She could apply all that she learned from people like Dasio and Brauneis and work toward a style that would capture the innocence, naiveté, and purity of the young child. We know that she sketched the young children who visited the grounds of the Siessen Convent frequently. And by looking at her drawings, one can see that her style was beginning to crystallize."

The Prolific Years: A Fusion of Religion and Art

Franciscan postulant Berta Hummel was given her habit of the Sisters of the Third Order of Saint Francis on August 20, 1934. As the presiding Bishop cut the symbolic lock of hair from her head, he bestowed upon her a new name: Sister Maria Innocentia. The feelings of innocence and veneration, traits identified strongly with the Franciscans, would come to play an important part in the artist's work.

That same year the artist's secular, and religious, work received a boost when the Siessen Convent agreed to allow the Munich-based publishers Ars Sacra to distribute Hummel art cards based on a variety of subjects throughout Germany and the rest of Europe. Also in 1934, *Das Hummelbuch*, a children's book illustrated by Sister Maria Innocentia Hummel with text by Mararette Seeman, published by the Emil Fink Publishing House in Stuttgart, appeared and was an immediate success.

"Though the themes of Sister Maria Innocentia's work are a primary reason for the artist's popularity it also should be said that color figures prominently in the appeal of this work," says Dr. Franz Julius Tschudy, a longtime editor at Ars Sacra (now Ars Edition) in Munich, who has been actively working on the publication of Hummel art cards for over three decades. "In essence, Sister Maria Innocentia was a purist when it came to color. She preferred muted colors for many of her works depicting children because the colors worked to create a timeless effect. Yet on some of her religious drawings she used brighter pastels to give the feeling of radiance and illumination."

Observing two of Sister Maria Innocentia's works, *Mary, Queen of May* and *Holy Franciscus* (this page, at right), both of which were done during the latter half of 1933, we can see how she used blues, reds, and yellows to create an illuminating effect. The art radiates in such a way that it resembles the stained glass images that appear in the windows of so many churches. Yet when looking at *Little Tailor* or *Latest News* (page 292), her use of muted colors is quite obvious. Her Easter cards, done during the summer of 1934 (pages 291-292, top), reflect a synthesis of these two styles, though the colors are sufficiently muted so as not to dominate.

During the mid and late 1930's, Sister Maria Innocentia worked

She was already starting to gain recognition as an important religious artist in 1933, when she completed Holy Franciscus, *an image of Saint Francis, top, and* Mary, Queen of May, *above.*

Opposite page: Loving Mother and Child *is one of Sister Maria Innocentia's more colorful religious works.*

frequently in charcoal and pastel chalks, sketching religious subjects, seasonal holiday cards and young children in traditional folk costumes. Occasionally she would draw in a large format, but most of her work during this period was postcard, or book, size, roughly the average size of an M.I. Hummel figurine. These were her most prolific years, very much to the delight of the growing audience who admired her images in the United States and in Europe.

In the United States, the smiling faces of Sister Maria Innocentia's children appealed to people who had endured nearly a decade of hard times through the Great Depression and the Dust Bowl years of the 1930's. America was full of slogans and images promoting the Roosevelt-era social programs that were designed to boost the morale of the average person; one in particular was the ultra-realistic WPA art that the government commissioned and placed in public buildings in cities around the country. And while *The Saturday Evening Post* covers and other works of Norman Rockwell helped promote basic American values, the M.I. Hummel figurines and art cards offered soft, innocent images that appealed to the average American on both the emotional and spiritual levels.

"Her art has mass appeal because of its universality," says Professor Dr. Gertz. "Almost everyone who came into contact with the figurines, or cards for that matter, could see just a little bit of themselves in her work—particularly in the faces and motifs. There is an anonymous emotional quality in those faces that rings true of childhood, naiveté and happier times."

Sister Maria Innocentia's work was also gaining popularity in Germany as well as in other German-speaking areas of central Europe including the Alsace and Lorraine regions of France, Austria, Switzerland and the Sudeten region of Czechoslovakia. Europe, like the United States, was emerging from a period of extreme economic hardship, and the themes prevalent in Sister Maria Innocentia's work at that time offered graphic indications of a new beginning. A feeling of extreme protection and shelter are inherent in the image of her *Loving Mother and Child* (page 288) done in July, 1937. The glowing colors evident in the wheels behind Mother Mary, and the look of hope in the face of the young child bid comfort and peace. In contrast, *Hautprobe (Little Scholar)* (page 292, top left) offers the somewhat startled, but earnest, image of a young schoolboy stepping out on his own for an important test in his young life. Once again, the artist's use of muted colors helps engage the viewer in the image.

But these themes, however universal and hopeful, ran against the prevailing thought of their time. Germany's Nazi government had taken note of the popularity of Sister Maria Innocentia's art, and had concluded that her work was not consistent with their goals. They took objection to Sister Maria Innocentia's art, and to the convent system of which she was clearly a part.

By 1937, the Nazis were putting the final touches on a systematic restructuring of the German education system in order to purge it of religious influence. Accordingly, religious schools were being forced to adopt Nazi doctrines and teaching methods. Special taxes were imposed on religious schools in order to weaken them financially and eventually force them out of operation. Siessen was one of many convents particulary hard-hit by this practice. Licensing fees that came from Sister Maria Innocentia's art were an important factor in the convent's ability to survive during these years.

These four cards were published as Easter cards (top left and right) and New Year cards (bottom left and right), by Ars Sacra. Collectors will recognize these themes as the bases for some of the M.I. Hummel figurines.

During 1937 Sister Maria Innocentia's art came under direct attack in the Nazi publication *SA-Mann*, with the comment that it did not uphold the values of the Nazi state. In 1938, her work came under attack again in the magazine *Hochland*, in an article entitled "Heresy in Pictures." The repressive tactics of the Nazi regime did not stop Sister Maria Innocentia from continuing with her work. She went on creating many new pieces of art in her studio on the second floor of the Siessen Convent. But during 1938, her health began to weaken.

Surviving the War Years

Sister Maria Innocentia's first seven years at Siessen had been prolific ones. Now, slowed by respiratory problems, she was often required to spend extended periods resting at the convent, or in nearby sanitoriums. It was only her strong will that enabled her to produce such works as *The Little Postman* (page 292, bottom left) bringing news of love, and *The Little Tailor* (page 292, top right) looking out with grave concern over his glasses. And at the outset of the Second World War, in September, 1939, she completed *Die Schmerzenmutter (Pieta)*, a strong emotional statement of the pain and suffering that was to come over the next several years.

In October, 1940, the situation at Siessen was further complicated with the expropriation of the convent by the Nazi government. The Nazis took over Siessen's farmland as well and sent all but forty of the two hundred and ninety sisters home to their families. Sister Maria Innocentia chose to be one of the small group of sisters who stayed on. The convent was turned into a repatriation center for ethnic Germans who had formerly resided in those countries that were now occupied by the Nazis. Food and living conditions were substandard, particularly the heating of the convent buildings. Medical supplies, as well as artists' materials, were hard to find.

That same year the Nazis issued orders that prohibited Ars Sacra from selling books and cards containing Sister Maria Innocentia's work in what was then known as "greater Germany." Ars Sacra was allowed to continue to make her work available in certain foreign countries, but was continually harassed by the Gestapo, who surveyed the publisher's offices under the pretense of investigating irregular currency transactions. In October of 1942, Sister Maria Innocentia wrote to Ars Sacra, expressing the feeling that the Nazis were trying to "hem me in."

Nevertheless, Sister Maria Innocentia continued to live and work at the Siessen Convent for the remainder of the war years. She drew when her health permitted, providing inspiration for the other sisters who stayed on at Siessen through these difficult times. Typical of this period of her work is *Slumber Time* (this page, above right), which she completed in September, 1943. A young boy lies in a garden hammock surrounded by flowers, a small bird, and the familiar bumblebee that she often used in her drawings. At the bottom is the inscription: "he dreams of better times." Toward the end of 1943 Hitler's armies were collapsing on the eastern front and it was becoming evident to most Germans that the tide of the war was shifting against them. This drawing of Sister Maria Innocentia's, created in a time of grave uncertainty, offered a glimmer of hope.

Succumbing to Illness

During the fall of 1944, Sister Maria Innocentia developed pleurisy, and this illness, according to those at Siessen and Ars Sacra who remember,

Above: Slumber Time *was drawn in September, 1943, after the Nazi's had expropriated the Siessen Convent.*

Opposite page: the four themes of the cards shown here are the bases for several M.I. Hummel figurines. Sister Maria Innocentia's use of muted colors is evident in each sketch. These drawings were done in the late 1930's, at the end of her most prolific period. Clockwise from top left: Little Scholar, Little Tailor, Latest News *and* The Postman.

Sister Maria Innocentia's Mainz Madonna and Child *is a classic example of the religious art tradition during the first half of the twentieth century. Often overlooked, Sister Maria Innocentia's religious art helps set a classical standard of this genre for our time.*

The Guardian Angel, shown at left, is a slight departure in style from most of Sister Maria Innocentia's religious drawings. It is indicative of what can be considered the contemporary style of her day.

Overleaf: Sister Maria Innocentia's drawing, Annunciation of Mary. *Her religious drawings were an important part of her work. As we can see in this work, she held to a tradition of religious art that developed over centuries of European cultural history.*

set off a series of other health problems. She had little strength for her art now, and during the winter of 1944-45 she lived in the Wilhelmstift Sanatorium in the Swabian town of Isny, where she was cared for by another Franciscan sister. She returned to Siessen in April of 1945, around the time the convent was liberated by French troops. Even though she was happy that her convent would resume normal operation, Sister Maria Innocentia had to contend with her pleurisy condition, which had developed into a full-scale tubercular lung infection.

Dr. Herbert Dubler, the head of Ars Sacra, offered to arrange for a bed at the Agra Sanatorium in the Swiss canton of Ticino, where the weather was generally mild, so that Sister Maria Innocentia might enjoy the benefits of the good climate. The artist considered this possibility, but her strength was simply at too low an ebb for her to make the journey through Switzerland. Instead, she went to the Wangen Sanatorium in the Swabian Allgau region, where she was cared for by sisters from Siessen.

In November, 1945, Sister Maria Innocentia's health came to the attention of the American military government in Germany. Aware of the popularity of her artwork in the United States during the years before America entered the war, the American military government made an important gesture of goodwill—they offered to provide a hospital plane to transfer Sister Maria Innocentia to an American military hospital where she could receive the benefits of American medical knowledge, or to any other hospital of her choosing. The offer, however, was not taken up. Sister Maria Innocentia remained near Siessen, instead.

"At the end of 1945, doctors gave her permission to draw again," remembers Ars Sacra's Dr. Tschudy. "And during the first half of 1946, while she was still at Wangen, we received news from Siessen telling us she had regained her lust to work."

This slight recovery did not last long. Sister Maria Innocentia returned to her beloved Siessen in the fall of 1946, but her condition worsened. The tubercular lung infection that sapped so much of her strength continued to weaken her, and on November 6, 1946, Sister Maria Innocentia Hummel died.

"When an artist passes on it often takes time for society to judge the impact of their work," says Professor Dr. Ulrich Gertz. "But the uninterrupted popularity of this artist's work over the past four decades leaves little question as to its appeal. The key to this broad-based appeal is the universality of the child and of the free spirit we have all had as children, which remains locked deep inside each and every one of us. Sister Maria Innocentia's use of color, emotion, and movement in her work is very classic. If we put her work into a time capsule for one hundred years, when that capsule is opened, her images will still be as strong and as valid as they are today."

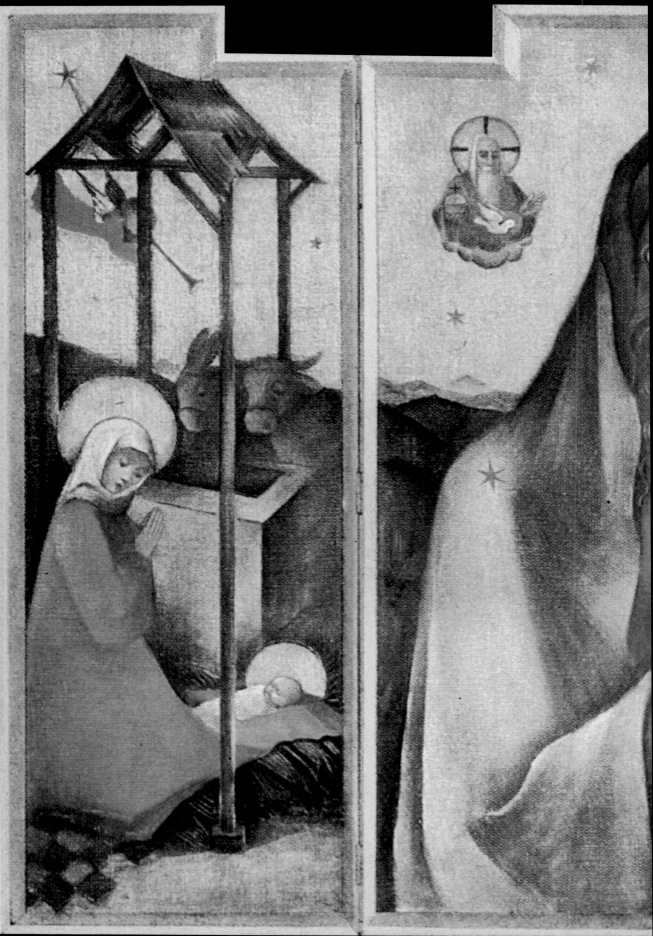

A History and Explanation of Marks and Symbols

A number of different marks have been used on the M.I. Hummel figurines since 1935. The "wide-crown-WG" trademark was used on the first figurines produced in 1935. On the earliest ones this mark was incised on the bottom of the base along with the "M.I. Hummel" signature on the top or side of the base. Between 1935 and 1955, the company occasionally used a © ⁓ mark on the side or top of the base of some models. This mark is sometimes seen to the right of the "M.I. Hummel" signature. The "crown" appears either incised or stamped. When both are used on the same piece, the mark is known as a "double crown." From 1946 through 1948, it was necessary to add the stamped words: "Made in the U.S. Zone Germany." This mark was used with various types of frames, or without a frame, underglazed or stamped over the glaze in black ink.

In 1950, four years after Sister Maria Innocentia Hummel's death, the Goebel company radically changed the trademark, as a tribute to her. The new trademark was a bee flying high in a "V." ("Hummel" means *bumblebee* in German, and the "V" stands for "Verkaufsgesellschaft" or *distribution company*.) The mark, known as the "full bee" trademark, was used until 1955 and appeared — sometimes both incised and underglazed — in black or blue and occasionally in green or magenta. In addition, the stamp "Germany," and later "West Germany," or "Western Germany," appeared. An (R) appearing beside the trademark stands for "Registered" and has no other significance.

Sometimes the molds were produced with a lightly incised circle on the bottom of the base in which the trademark was centered. The circle has no significance other than as a target for the location of the decal. Some current production figurines still have this incised circle.

The company continued to modify the trademark through the 1950's; in 1956, they made the bee smaller, with its wing tips parallel with the top of the "V" (it was still inside the "V"). In 1957, the bee rose slightly above the "V." In 1958, the bee became even smaller and it flew deep within the "V." The year 1959 saw the beginning of stylization and the wings of the bee became sharply angular.

In 1960, the completely stylized bee with "V" mark came into use, appearing with "W. Germany." This mark was used, in one form or another, until 1979. In addition to its appearance with "W. Germany" to the right of the mark (1960-1963), it appeared centered above the "W. Germany" (1960-1972), and to the left of the "three line mark" (mid-1960's to 1972). The three line mark was used intermittently, and sometimes concurrently, with the small, stylized 1960-72 mark. It was the most prominent trademark in use prior to the "Goebel bee."

It eventually became apparent that the public was equating the "V and Bee" mark only with M.I. Hummel items and did not realize that it included the full scope of Goebel products. The company experimented further with marks and in 1972 began using a printed "Goebel" with the stylized bee poised between the letters "b" and "e."

Since 1976, the Goebel trademark on M.I. Hummel figurines has been affixed by a decal on top of the glaze. Prior to that time, it was always under the glaze. It is possible for two figurines on the primary market to have differing decals.

In 1979, the stylized bee was dropped and since then, only the name Goebel appears. That same year, for the first time, the year of production was hand-lettered on the base next to the initials of the chief decorator.

Note: While these are all the Goebel trademarks currently known to be authorized for use on M.I. Hummel figurines, it is always possible that a few rare and undocumented variations may exist.

306

1935-1949

Incised Crown

1935-1955

Stamped Crown

1946-1948

1950-1955

Incised

Stamped

Stamped

Full Bee

Full Bee

W. GOEBEL

1956

Small Bee

1957

High Bee

1958

Baby Bee

1959

V Bee

1957-1960

Early Stylized (Incised Circle)

1935-1955

Germany

West Germany

Western Germany

GERMANY

Western
Germany

© W. Goebel

Copr. W. Goebel

1960-1963

1960-1972

1964-1972

1972-1979

1979 Current Trademark

Name	HUM Number	Shown on page(s)
Sad Song	**404**	123
Saint George	**55**	155, 281
School Boy	**82**	58, 98
School Boys	**170**	92
School Girl	**81**	98
School Girls	**177**	93
Sensitive Hunter	**6**	84
Serenade	**85**	125
She Loves Me, She Loves Me Not!	**174**	83, 275
Shepherd Boy	**395**	
Shepherd's Boy	**64**	85
Shining Light	**358**	143
Signs Of Spring	**203**	175
Sing Along	**433**	114
Singing Angel, *see* **Christmas Song**	**343**	140
Singing Lesson	**63**	81, 82
Sing With Me	**405**	90
Sister	**98**	86, 104
Sisterly Love, *see* **Daddy's Girls**	**371**	85
Skier	**59**	137
Sleep Tight	**424**	118
Slumber Serenade, *see* **Sunny Morning**	**313**	116
Smart Little Sister	**346**	74, 82
Smiling Through	**408**	59
Soldier Boy	**332**	56
Soloist	**135**	124
Spring Bouquet	**398**	90
Spring Cheer	**72**	115, 274
Spring Dance	**353**	132-133
Star Gazer	**132**	74
Stitch In Time	**255**	120
Stormy Weather	**71**	48
Street Singer	**131**	124
Strolling Along	**5**	61
Sunny Morning	**313**	116
Supreme Protection	**364**	152
Suprise	**94**	57
Sweet Greetings	**352**	104
Sweet Music	**186**	128
Telling Her Secret	**196**	177
The Artist	**304**	174
The Botanist	**351**	85
The Builder	**305**	103
The Fisherman, *see* **Just Fishing**	**373**	85

Name	HUM Number	Shown on page(s)
Which Hand?	**258**	57
Whistler's Duet	**413**	79
Whitsuntide	**163**	143
With Loving Greetings	**309**	138
Worship	**84**	157
Young Shepherd, see **Shepherd Boy**	**395**	
Unnamed at publication time	**437**	
Unnamed at publication time	**438**	147
Unnamed at publication time	**447**	123

International Designs

Name	HUM Number	Shown on page(s)
Bulgarian-Style	**807, 809, 810**	270
Czech-Style	**841, 842**	269
Hungarian-Style	**851, 852, 853, 854**	270
Serbian-Style	**812, 904, 913 947, 968**	270
Slovak-Style	**831, 832**	269
Swedish-Style	**824, 825**	269

Annual Bells

Name	HUM Number	Shown on page(s)
Let's Sing, 1978	**700**	165
Farewell, 1979	**701**	165
Thoughtful, 1980	**702**	165
In Tune, 1981	**703**	165
She Loves Me, 1982	**704**	165
Knit One, 1983	**705**	165
Mountaineer, 1984	**706**	165
Girl With Sheet Of Music, 1985	**707**	165
Sing Along, 1986	**708**	165
With Loving Greetings, 1987	**709**	165
Busy Student, 1988	**710**	165
Latest News, 1989	**711**	165
What's New? 1990	**712**	165

Anniversary Bell

Name	HUM Number	Shown on page(s)
Just Resting, 1985	**730**	

Annual Plates

Name	HUM Number	Shown on page(s)
Heavenly Angel, 1971	**264**	166
Hear Ye, Hear Ye, 1972	**265**	166
Globe Trotter, 1973	**266**	166
Goose Girl, 1974	**267**	166
Ride Into Christmas, 1975	**268**	166
Apple Tree Girl, 1976	**269**	167

Name	HUM Number	Shown on page(s)
Apple Tree Boy, 1977	270	166
Happy Pastime, 1978	271	167
Singing Lesson, 1979	272	167
School Girl, 1980	273	167
Umbrella Boy, 1981	274	167
Umbrella Girl, 1982	275	167
Postman, 1983	276	166
Little Helper, 1984	277	166
Chick Girl, 1985	278	166
Playmates, 1986	279	166
Feeding Time, 1987	283	166
Little Goat Herder, 1988	284	167
Farm Boy, 1989	285	166
Shepherd's Boy, 1990	286	167
Just Resting, 1991	287	167
Wayside Harmony, 1992	288	167

Anniversary Plates

Name	HUM Number	Shown on page(s)
Stormy Weather, 1975	280	164
Pair of girls from Ring Around The Rosie (Spring Dance), 1980	281	164
Auf Wiedersehn, 1985	282	164
Mother's Day Plate	500	

Ashtrays

Name	HUM Number	Shown on page(s)
Boy With Bird	166	166
Happy Pastime	62	169
Joyful	33	169
Joyful (without rest for cigarette)	216 (CN – never released)	
Let's Sing	114	169
Singing Lesson	34	169

Bookends

Name	HUM Number	Shown on page(s)
Apple Tree Girl & Apple Tree Boy	252A & 252B	84
Book Worm Boy & Book Worm Girl	14A & 14B	86-97
Doll Mother & Prayer Before Battle	76A & 76B	
Eventide & Adoration (without shrine)	90A & 90B	
Farm Boy & Goose Girl	60A & 60 B	89
Good Friends & She Loves Me, She Loves Me Not!	251A & 251B	90
Joyful and Let's Sing	120	90
Little Goat Herder & Feeding Time	250A & 250B	84

Name	HUM Number	Shown on page(s)
Playmates & Chick Girl	**61A & 61B**	89
Puppy Love and Serenade With Dog	**122**	
Wayside Harmony and Just Resting	**121**	

Candleholders

Name	HUM Number	Shown on page(s)
Angel Duet	**193**	147, 171
Angelic Sleep	**25**	147
Angel Lights	**241**	145
Begging His Share (before 1964)	**9**	
Birthday Cake	**338**	139, 277
Boy With Horse	**117**	140
Candlelight	**192**	144, 278
Girl With Fir Tree	**116**	140
Girl With Nosegay	**115**	140
Heavenly Song	**113**	278
Herald Angels	**37**	278
Joyous News	**271**	
Joyous News, Angel With Accordion	**39**	
Joyous News, Angel With Lute	**38**	
Joyous News, Angel With Trumpet	**49**	
Little Band	**388**	135
Lullaby	**24**	170
Silent Night	**54**	142, 278
Silent Night With Black Child	**31**	278

Candy Boxes

Name	HUM Number	Shown on page(s)
Chick Girl	**111/57**	169
Happy Pastime	**111/69**	169
Happy Pastime (old style)	**221 (CN — never released)**	
Joyful	**111/53**	169
Let's Sing	**111/110**	169
Playmates	**111/58**	169
Singing Lesson	**111/63**	169

Clocks

Name	HUM Number	Shown on page(s)
Call To Worship	**441**	171
Chapel Time	**442**	173
Country Song	**443**	172

Holy Water Fonts

Name	HUM Number	Shown on page(s)
Angel Cloud	**206**	158
Angel Duet	**146**	158
Angel Facing Left	**91A**	158

Name	HUM Number	Shown on page(s)
Angel Facing Right	91B	158
Angel, Joyous News	242	
Angel Shrine	147	158
Angel With Bird	167	158
Angel With Birds	22	158
Angel With Cross and Bird	354C	
Angel With Lantern	354A	
Angel With Lute	241	
Angel With Trumpet	354B	
Child Jesus	26	158
Child With Flowers	36	158
Dove	393	158
Guardian Angel	29	
Guardian Angel	248	158
Heavenly Angel	207	158
Holy Cross	77	
Holy Family	246	158
Madonna and Child	243	158
Sitting Angel	22	
The Good Shepherd	35	158
White Angel	75	158
Worship	164	158

Music Boxes

Name	HUM Number	Shown on page(s)
Little Band on Music Box	392M	
Little Band, Candleholder on Music Box	388M	135

Nativity Sets — Components

Name	HUM Number	Shown on page(s)
Large Nativity Set With Wooden Stable	260	150-151
Angel Serenade	260E	141, 151
Cow, lying	260M	150
Donkey, standing	260L	150
Good Night	260D	150
Infant Jesus	260C	151
King, kneeling	260P	
King, standing	260O	151
Little Tooter	260K	150
Madonna	260A	151
Moorish King, standing	260N	151
One Sheep, lying	260R	150
Saint Joseph	260B	151
Sheep, standing with lamb	260H	150
Shepherd Boy, kneeling	260J	150
Shepherd, standing	260G	150

Name	HUM Number	Shown on page(s)
We Congratulate	260F	151
Nativity Set With Wooden Stable	214	148-149
Angel, kneeling, Angel Serenade	214D	148
Good Night	214C	149
Donkey	214J	148
Flying Angel	366	148
Infant Jesus	214A	149
Joseph	214B	148
King, kneeling	214M	149
King, kneeling, with cash-box	214N	149
Lamb	214O	149, 149
Madonna and Child	214A	281
Moorish King	214L	149
Ox	214K	148
Shepherd, kneeling	214G	148
Shepherd, kneeling with flute, Little Tooter	214H	148
Shepherd, standing	214F	148
Virgin Mary	214A	149
We Congratulate	214E	149, 273

Plaques

Name	HUM Number	Shown on page(s)
Ba-Bee Ring	30A & 30B	162
Being Punished	326	73
Child in Bed, Wall Plaque	137	162, 266
Flitting Butterfly	139	162, 266
Happy Bugler, see Tuneful Goodnight	180	161, 266
Little Fiddler	93	164
Little Fiddler (wood frame)	107	264
Madonna and Child (in relief)	249	
Madonna Plaque	48	159
Madonna Plaque (metal frame)	222	
Merry Christmas	323	160
Merry Wanderer	92	164
Merry Wanderer(wood frame)	106	264
Merry Wanderer (in relief)	263	263
M.I. Hummel Store Plaques:		
In English	187	264
Redesigned from older model	187A	
Schmid	210	265
In English, Oeslau	211	265
In French	208	164
In German	205	
In Spanish	213	264
In Swedish	209	264
Quartet	134	164

Name	HUM Number	Shown on page(s)
Retreat To Safety	**126**	164
Searching Angel	**310**	160
Smiling Through, Goebel Collectors' Club Plaque	**690**	168
Standing Boy	**168**	164
Star Gazer	**237**	
Swaying Lullaby	**165**	163
The Mail Is Here	**140**	164
Tiny Baby In Crib	**138**	266
Tuneful Goodnight	**180**	161, 266
Vacation Time	**125**	164
Wall picture with sitting woman and child	**156**	

Table Lamps

Name	HUM Number	Shown on page(s)
Apple Tree Boy	**230**	
Apple Tree Girl	**229**	134
Birthday Serenade	**231, 234**	276, 134
Culprits	**44A**	134
Eventide	**104**	276
Farewell	**103**	277
Good Friends	**228**	
Happy Days	**232, 235**	134
Just Resting	**11/112, 225**	
Old Man Reading Newspaper	**202**	268
Out Of Danger	**44B**	
She Loves Me, She Loves Me Not!	**227**	134
Shrine	**100**	276
To Market	**101, 223**	276, 135
Volunteers	**102**	277
Wayside Harmony	**11/111,224**	

Wall Vases

Name	HUM Number	Shown on page(s)
Boy and Girl	**360A**	
Boy	**360B**	
Girl	**360C**	

"Mel" Signature Items		266
Norman Rockwell Items		267
The Flying Bumblebee		267
Walt Disney Items		267